American Measures
Three Centuries
of American
Poetry

Published by Lowe & B. Hould Publishers,®
an imprint of Borders, Inc.
311 Maynard, Ann Arbor, MI 48104
All rights reserved

Lowe & B. Hould Publishers is a
registered trademark of Borders Properties, Inc.

ISBN 0-681-05563-4

10 9 8 7 6 5 4 3 2 1

Printed and bound in the
United States of America

Designed by Mike Savitski,
Ann Arbor, Michigan

Contents

Edna St. Vincent Millay (1892–1950)

ANNE BRADSTREET

c. 1612–1672

The Prologue

1

To sing of wars, of captains, and of kings,
Of cities founded, commonwealths begun,
For my mean pen are too superior things:
Or how they all, or each their dates have run
Let poets and historians set these forth,
My obscure lines shall not so dim their worth.

2

But when my wond'ring eyes and envious heart
Great Bartas' sugared lines do but read o'er,
Fool I do grudge the Muses did not part
'Twixt him and me that overfluent store;
A Bartas can do what a Bartas will
But simple I according to my skill.

3

From schoolboy's tongue no rhet'ric we expect,
Nor yet a sweet consort from broken strings,
Nor perfect beauty where's a main defect:
My foolish, broken, blemished Muse so sings,
And this to mend, alas, no art is able,
'Cause nature made it so irreparable.

4

Nor can I, like that fluent sweet tongued Greek,
Who lisped at first, in future times speak plain.
By art he gladly found what he did seek,
A full requital of his striving pain.
Art can do much, but this maxim's most sure:
A weak or wounded brain admits no cure.

5

I am obnoxious to each carping tongue
Who says my hand a needle better fits,
A poet's pen all scorn I should thus wrong;
For such despite they cast on female wits:
If what I do prove well, it won't advance,
They'll say it's stol'n, or else it was by chance.

6

But sure the antique Greeks were far more mild
Else of our sex, why feigned they those nine
And poesy made Calliope's own child;
So 'mongst the rest they placed the arts divine:
But this weak knot they will full soon untie,
The Greeks did nought, but play the fools and lie.

7

Let Greeks be Greeks, and women what they are
Men have precedency and still excel,
It is but vain unjustly to wage war;
Men can do best, and women know it well.
Preeminence in all and each is yours;
Yet grant some small acknowledgement of ours.

8

And oh ye high flown quills that soar the skies,
And ever with your prey still catch your praise,
If e'er you deign these lowly lines your eyes,
Give thyme or parsley wreath, I ask no bays;
This mean and unrefined ore of mine
Will make your glist'ring gold but more to shine.

The Author to Her Book

Thou ill-formed offspring of my feeble brain,
Who after birth didst by my side remain,
Till snatched from thence by friends, less wise than true,
Who thee abroad, exposed to public view,
Made thee in rags, halting to th' press to trudge,
Where errors were not lessened (all my judge).
At thy return my blushing was not small,
My rambling brat (in print) should mother call,
I cast thee by as one unfit for light,
Thy visage was so irksome in my sight;
Yet being mine own, at length affection would
Thy blemishes amend, if so I could:
I washed thy face, but more defects I saw,

And rubbing off a spot still made a flaw.
I stretched thy joints to make thee even feet,
Yet still thou run'st more hobbling than is meet;
In better dress to trim thee was my mind,
But nought save homespun cloth i' th' house I find.
In this array 'mongst vulgars may'st thou roam.
In critic's hands beware thou dost not come,
And take thy way where yet thou art not known;
If for thy father asked, say thou hadst none;
And for thy mother, she alas is poor,
Which caused her thus to send thee out of door.

Deliverance from a Fit of Fainting

Worthy art Thou, O Lord, of praise,
  But ah! It's not in me.
My sinking heart I pray Thee raise
  So shall I give it Thee.

My life as spider's webb's cut off,
  Thus fainting have I said,
And living man no more shall see
  But be in silence laid.

My feeble spirit Thou didst revive,
  My doubting Thou didst chide,
And though as dead mad'st me alive,
  I here a while might 'bide.

Why should I live but to Thy praise?
  My life is hid with Thee.
O Lord, no longer be my days
  Than I may fruitful be.

A Letter to Her Husband, Absent upon Public Employment

My head, my heart, mine eyes, my life, nay, more,
My joy, my magazine of earthly store,
If two be one, as surely thou and I,
How stayest thou there, whilst I at Ipswich lie?
So many steps, head from the heart to sever,
If but a neck, soon should we be together.
I, like the Earth this season, mourn in black,
My Sun is gone so far in's zodiac,
Whom whilst I 'joyed, nor storms, nor frost I felt,
His warmth such frigid colds did cause to melt.
My chilled limbs now numbed lie forlorn;
Return; return, sweet Sol, from Capricorn;
In this dead time, alas, what can I more
Than view those fruits which through thy heat I bore?
Which sweet contentment yield me for a space,
True living pictures of their father's face.
O strange effect! now thou art southward gone,
I weary grow the tedious day so long;
But when thou northward to me shalt return,
I wish my Sun may never set, but burn
Within the Cancer of my glowing breast,
The welcome house of him my dearest guest.
Where ever, ever stay, and go not thence,
Till nature's sad decree shall call thee hence;
Flesh of thy flesh, bone of thy bone,
I here, thou there, yet both but one.

To My Dear and Loving Husband

If ever two were one, then surely we.
If ever man were loved by wife, then thee;
If ever wife was happy in a man,
Compare with me, ye women, if you can.
I prize thy love more than whole mines of gold
Or all the riches that the East doth hold.
My love is such that rivers cannot quench,
Nor ought but love from thee, give recompense.
Thy love is such I can no way repay,
The heavens reward thee manifold, I pray.
Then while we live, in love let's so persevere
That when we live no more, we may live ever.

Before the Birth of One of Her Children

All things within this fading world hath end,
Adversity doth still our joys attend;
No ties so strong, no friends so dear and sweet,
But with death's parting blow is sure to meet.
The sentence past is most irrevocable,
A common thing, yet oh, inevitable.
How soon, my Dear, death may my steps attend,
How soon't may be thy lot to lose thy friend,
We both are ignorant, yet love bids me
These farewell lines to recommend to thee,
That when that knot's untied that made us one,
I may seem thine, who in effect am none.
And if I see not half my days that's due,
What nature would, God grant to yours and you;
The many faults that well you know I have

Let be interred in my oblivious grave;
If any worth or virtue were in me,
Let that live freshly in thy memory
And when thou feel'st no grief, as I no harms,
Yet love thy dead, who long lay in thine arms.
And when thy loss shall be repaid with gains
Look to my little babes, my dear remains.
And if thou love thyself, or loved'st me,
These O protect from step-dame's injury.
And if chance to thine eyes shall bring this verse,
With some sad sighs honour my absent hearse;
And kiss this paper for thy love's dear sake,
Who with salt tears this last farewell did take.

Here Follows Some Verses upon the Burning of Our House July 10th, 1666

Copied Out of a Loose Paper

In silent night when rest I took
For sorrow near I did not look
I wakened was with thund'ring noise
And piteous shrieks of dreadful voice.
That fearful sound of "Fire!" and "Fire!"
Let no man know is my desire.
I, starting up, the light did spy,
And to my God my heart did cry
To strengthen me in my distress
And not to leave me succorless.
Then, coming out, beheld a space
The flame consume my dwelling place.
And when I could no longer look,
I blest His name that gave and took,

That laid my goods now in the dust.
Yea, so it was, and so 'twas just.
It was His own, it was not mine,
Far be it that I should repine;
He might of all justly bereft
But yet sufficient for us left.
When by the ruins oft I past
My sorrowing eyes aside did cast,
And here and there the places spy
Where oft I sat and long did lie;
Here stood that trunk, and there that chest,
There lay that store I counted best.
My pleasant things in ashes lie,
And them behold no more shall I.
Under thy roof no guest shall sit,
Nor at thy table eat a bit.
No pleasant tale shall e'er be told,
Nor things recounted done of old.
No candle e'er shall shine in thee,
Nor bridegroom's voice e'er heard shall be.
In silence ever shall thou lie,
Adieu, Adieu, all's vanity.
Then straight I 'gin my heart to chide,
And did thy wealth on earth abide?
Didst fix thy hope on mold'ring dust?
The arm of flesh didst make thy trust?
Raise up thy thoughts above the sky
That dunghill mists away may fly.
Thou hast an house on high erect,
Framed by that mighty Architect,
With glory richly furnished,
Stands permanent though this be fled.
It's purchaséd and paid for too

By Him who hath enough to do.
A price so vast as is unknown
Yet by His gift is made thine own;
There's wealth enough, I need no more,
Farewell, my pelf, farewell my store.
The world no longer let me love,
My hope and treasure lies above.

In Memory of My Dear Grandchild Elizabeth Bradstreet, Who Deceased August, 1665, Being a Year and Half Old

1

Farewell dear babe, my heart's too much content,
Farewell sweet babe, the pleasure of mine eye,
Farewell fair flower that for a space was lent,
Then ta'en away unto eternity.
Blest babe, why should I once bewail thy fate,
Or sigh thy days so soon were terminate,
Sith thou art settled in an everlasting state.

2

By nature trees do rot when they are grown,
And plums and apples thoroughly ripe do fall,
And corn and grass are in their season mown,
And time brings down what is both strong and tall.
But plants new set to be eradicate,
And buds new blown to have so short a date,
Is by His hand alone that guides nature and fate.

On My Dear Grandchild Simon Bradstreet Who Died on 16 November, 1669, Being But a Month, and One Day Old

No sooner came, but gone, and fall'n asleep,
Acquaintance short, yet parting caused us weep;
Three flowers, two scarcely blown, the last i' th' bud,
Cropt by th' Almighty's hand; yet is He good.
With dreadful awe before Him let's be mute,
Such was His will, but why, let's not dispute,
With humble hearts and mouths put in the dust,
Let's say He's merciful as well as just.
He will return and make up all our losses,
And smile again after our bitter crosses
Go pretty babe, go rest with sisters twain;
Among the blest in endless joys remain.

As Weary Pilgrim

As weary pilgrim, now at rest,
    Hugs with delight his silent nest,
His wasted limbs now lie full soft
    That mirey steps have trodden oft,
Blesses himself to think upon
    His dangers past, and travails done.
The burning sun no more shall heat,
    Nor stormy rains on him shall beat.
The briars and thorns no more shall scratch,
    Nor hungry wolves at him shall catch.
He erring paths no more shall tread,
    Nor wild fruits eat instead of bread.

For waters cold he doth not long
　　For thirst no more shall parch his tongue.
No rugged stones his feet shall gall,
　　Nor stumps nor rocks cause him to fall.
All cares and fears he bids farewell
　　And means in safety now to dwell.
A pilgrim I, on earth perplexed
　　With sins, with cares and sorrows vext,
By age and pains brought to decay,
　　And my clay house mold'ring away.
Oh, how I long to be at rest
　　And soar on high among the blest.
This body shall in silence sleep,
　　Mine eyes no more shall ever weep,
No fainting fits shall me assail,
　　Nor grinding pains my body frail,
With cares and fears ne'er cumb'red be
　　Nor losses know, nor sorrows see,
What though my flesh shall there consume,
　　It is the bed Christ did perfume,
And when a few years shall be gone,
　　This mortal shall be clothed upon.
A corrupt carcass down it lays,
　　A glorious body it shall rise:
In weakness and dishonour sown,
　　In power 'tis raised by Christ alone.
Then soul and body shall unite
　　And of their Maker have the sight.
Such lasting joys shall there behold
　　As ear ne'er heard nor tongue e'er told.
Lord make me ready for that day,
　　Then come, dear Bridegroom, come away.

The Flesh and the Spirit

In secret place where once I stood
Close by by the banks of Lacrim flood,
I heard two sisters reason on
Things that are past and things to come;
One flesh was called, who had her eye
On wordly wealth and vanity;
The other Spirit, who did rear
Her thoughts unto a higher sphere:
Sister, quoth Flesh, what liv'st thou on,
Nothing but meditation?
Doth contemplation feed thee so
Regardlessly to let earth go?
Can speculation satisfy
Notion without reality?
Dost dream of things beyond the moon,
And dost thou hope to dwell there soon?
Hast treasures there laid up in store
That all in th' world thou count'st but poor?
Art fancy sick, or turned a sot
To catch at shadows which are not?
Come, come, I'll show unto thy sense,
Industry hath its recompense.
What canst desire, but thou may'st see
True substance in variety?
Dost honor like? Acquire the same,
As some to their immortal fame,
And trophies to thy name erect
Which wearing time shall ne'er deject.
For riches doth thou long full sore?
Behold enough of precious store.
Earth hath more silver, pearls, and gold,

Than eyes can see or hands can hold.
Affect's thou pleasure? Take thy fill,
Earth hath enough of what you will.
Then let not go, what thou may'st find
For things unknown, only in mind.

Spirit: Be still thou unregenerate part,
Disturb no more my settled heart,
For I have vowed (and so will do)
There as a foe still to pursue.
And combat with thee will and must,
Until I see thee laid in th' dust.
Sisters we are, yea, twins we be,
Yet deadly feud 'twixt thee and me;
For from one father are we not,
Thou by old Adam wast begot.
But my arise is from above,
Whence my dear Father I do love.
Thou speak'st me fair, but hat'st me sore,
Thy flatt'ring shows I'll trust no more.
How oft thy slave, hast thou me made,
When I believed what thou hast said,
And never had more cause of woe
Than when I did what thou bad'st do.
I'll stop mine ears at these thy charms,
And count them for my deadly harms.
Thy sinful pleasures I do hate,
Thy riches are to me no bait,
Thine honors do, nor will I love;
For my ambition lies above.
My greatest honor it shall be
When I am victor over thee,
And triumph shall with laurel head,

When thou my captive shalt be led,
How I do live, thou need'st not scoff,
For I have meat thou know'st not of;
The hidden manna I do eat,
The word of life it is my meat.
My thoughts do yield me more content.
Than can thy hours in pleasure spent.
Nor are they shadows which I catch,
Nor fancies vain at which I snatch,
But reach at things that are so high,
Beyond thy dull capacity;
Eternal substance I do see,
With which enrichéd I would be.
Mine eye doth pierce the heavens and see
What is invisible to thee.
My garments are not silk nor gold,
Nor such like trash which earth doth hold,
But royal robes I shall have on,
More glorious than the glist'ring sun;
My crown not diamonds, pearls, and gold,
But such as angels' heads enfold.
The city where I hope to dwell,
There's none on earth can parallel;
The stately walls both high and strong,
Are made of precious jasper stone;
The gates of pearl, both rich and clear,
And angels are for porters there;
The streets thereof transparent gold
Such as no eye did e'er behold;
A crystal river there doth run,
Which doth proceed from the Lamb's throne.
Of life, there are the waters sure,
Which shall remain forever pure,

Nor sun, nor moon, they have no need,
For glory doth from God proceed.
No candle there, nor yet torchlight,
For there shall be no darksome night.
From sickness and infirmity
For evermore they shall be free;
Nor withering age shall e'er come there,
But beauty shall be bright and clear;
This city pure is not for thee,
For things unclean there shall not be,
If I of heaven may have my fill,
Take thou the world and all that will.

EDWARD TAYLOR

c. 1642-1729

Huswifery

Make me, O Lord, thy spinning wheel complete.
　　Thy Holy Word my distaff make for me.
Make mine affections thy swift flyers neat
　　And make my soul thy holy spool to be.
　　My conversation make to be thy reel
　　And reel the yarn thereon spun of thy wheel.

Make me thy loom then, knit therein this twine.
　　And make thy Holy Spirit, Lord, wind quills:
Then weave the web thyself. The yarn is fine.
　　Thine ordinances make my fulling mills.
　　Then dye the same in heavenly colors choice,
　　All pinked with varnished flowers of paradise.

Then clothe therewith mine understanding, will,
　　Affections, judgment, conscience, memory
My words, and actions, that their shine may fill
　　My ways with glory and thee glorify.
　　Then mine apparel shall display before ye
　　That I am clothed in holy robes for glory.

Meditation 22 (First Series)

Philippians 2.9. God hath highly exalted him.

When thy bright beams, my Lord, do strike mine eye,
　　Methinks I then could truly chide outright
My hide-bound soul that stands so niggardly
　　That scarce a thought gets glorified by't.
　　My quaintest metaphors are ragged stuff,
　　Making the sun seem like a mullipuff.

It's my desire, Thou shouldst be glorified:
    But when Thy glory shines before mine eye,
I pardon crave, lest my desire be pride.
    Or bed Thy glory in a cloudy sky.
    The sun grows wan; and angels palefaced shrink,
    Before Thy shine, which I besmear with ink.

But shall the bird sing forth Thy praise, and shall
    The little bee present her thankful hum?
But I who see Thy shining glory fall
    Before mine eyes, stand blockish, dull, and dumb?
    Whether I speak, or speechless stand, I spy,
    I fail Thy glory: therefore pardon cry.

But this I find; my rhymes do better suit
    Mine own dispraise than tune forth praise to Thee.
Yet being child, whether consonant, or mute,
    I force my tongue to tattle, as You see.
    That I Thy glorious praise may trumpet right,
    Be thou my song, and make, Lord, me thy pipe.

This shining sky will fly away apace,
    When Thy bright glory splits the same to make
Thy majesty a pass, whose fairest face
    Too foul a path is for Thy feet to take.
    What glory then, shall tend Thee through the sky
    Draining the heaven much of angels dry?

What light then flame will in Thy judgment seat,
    'Fore which all men and angels shall appear?
How shall Thy glorious righteousness them treat,
    Rend'ring to each after his works done here?
    Then saints with angels thou wilt glorify:
    And burn lewd men, and devils gloriously.

One glimpse, my Lord, of Thy bright judgment day,
  And glory piercing through, like fiery darts,
All devils, doth me make for grace to pray,
    For filling grace had I ten thousand hearts.
    I'd through ten hells to see Thy judgment day
    Wouldst Thou but gild my soul with Thy bright ray.

PHILIP FRENEAU
1752-1832

The Wild Honey Suckle

Fair flower, that dost so comely grow,
Hid in this silent, dull retreat,
Untouched thy honied blossoms blow,
Unseen thy little branches greet:
    No roving foot shall crush thee here,
    No busy hand provoke a tear.

By Nature's self in white arrayed,
She bade thee shun the vulgar eye,
And planted here the guardian shade,
And sent soft waters murmuring by;
    Thus quietly thy summer goes,
    Thy days declining to repose.

Smit with those charms, that must decay,
I grieve to see your future doom;
They died—nor were those flowers more gay,
The flowers that did in Eden bloom;
    Unpitying frosts, and Autumn's power
    Shall leave no vestige of this flower.

From morning suns and evening dews
At first thy little being came;
If nothing once, you nothing lose,
For when you die you are the same;
    The space between, is but an hour,
    The frail duration of a flower.

On the Emigration to America and Peopling the Western Country

To western woods, and lonely plains,
Palemon from the crowd departs,
Where Nature's wildest genius reigns,
To tame the soil, and plant the arts—
What wonders there shall freedom show,
What mighty states successive grow!

From Europe's proud, despotic shores
Hither the stranger takes his way,
And in our new found world explores
A happier soil, a milder sway,
Where no proud despot holds him down,
No slaves insult him with a crown.

What charming scenes attract the eye,
On wild Ohio's savage stream!
There Nature reigns, whose works outvie
The boldest pattern art can frame;
There ages past have rolled away,
And forests bloomed but to decay.

From these fair plains, these rural seats,
So long concealed, so lately known,
The unsocial Indian far retreats,
To make some other clime his own,
When other streams, less pleasing flow,
And darker forests round him grow.

Great sire of floods! whose varied wave
Through climes and countries takes its way,
To whom creating Nature gave
Ten thousand streams to swell thy sway!
No longer shall they useless prove,
Nor idly through the forests rove;

Nor longer shall your princely flood
From distant lakes be swelled in vain,
Nor longer through a darksome wood
Advance, unnoticed, to the main,
Far other ends, the heavens decree—
And commerce plans new freights for thee.

While virtue warms the generous breast,
There heaven-born freedom shall reside,
Nor shall the voice of war molest,
Nor Europe's all-aspiring pride—
There Reason shall new laws devise,
And order from confusion rise.

Forsaking kings and regal state,
With all their pomp and fancied bliss,
The traveler owns, convinced though late,
No realm so free, so blessed as this—
The east is half to slaves consigned,
Where kings and priests enchain the mind.

O come the time, and haste the day,
When man shall man no longer crush,
When Reason shall enforce her sway,
Nor these fair regions raise our blush,
Where still the African complains,
And mourns his yet unbroken chains.

Far brighter scenes a future age,
The muse predicts, these states will hail,
Whose genius may the world engage,
Whose deeds may over death prevail,
And happier systems bring to view,
Than all the eastern sages knew.

The Indian Burying Ground

In spite of all the learned have said,
I still my old opinion keep;
The *posture,* that *we* give the dead,
Points out the soul's eternal sleep.

Not so the ancients of these lands—
The Indian, when from life released,
Again is seated with his friends,
And shares again the joyous feast.

His imaged birds, and painted bowl,
And venison, for a journey dressed,
Bespeak the nature of the soul,
ACTIVITY, that knows no rest.

His bow, for action ready bent,
And arrows, with a head of stone,
Can only mean that life is spent,
And not the old ideas gone.

Thou, stranger, that shalt come this way,
No fraud upon the dead commit—
Observe the swelling turf, and say
They do not *lie,* but here they *sit.*

Here still a lofty rock remains,
On which the curious eye may trace
(Now wasted, half, by wearing rains)
The fancies of a ruder race.

Here still an aged elm aspires,
Beneath whose far-projecting shade
(And which the shepherd still admires)
The children of the forest played!

There oft a restless Indian queen
(Pale *Shebah,* with her braided hair)
And many a barbarous form is seen
To chide the man that lingers there.

By midnight moons, o'er moistening dews,
In habit for the chase arrayed,
The hunter still the deer pursues,
The hunter and the deer, a shade!

And long shall timorous fancy see
The painted chief, and pointed spear,
And Reason's self shall bow the knee
To shadows and delusions here.

The American Soldier
(A Picture from the Life)

To serve with love,
And shed your blood,
Approved may be above,
And here below
(Examples shew)
'Tis dangerous to be good.
                    LORD OXFORD

Deep in a vale, a stranger now to arms,
Too poor to shine in courts, too proud to beg,
He, who once warred on Saratoga's plains,
Sits musing o'er his scars, and wooden leg.

Remembering still the toil of former days,
To *other* hands he sees his earnings paid;—
They share the due reward—*he* feeds on praise,
Lost in the abyss of want, misfortune's shade.

Far, far from domes where splendid tapers glare,
'Tis his from dear bought peace no wealth to win,
Removed alike from courtly cringing 'squires,
The great-man's *Levee,* and the proud man's grin.

Sold are those arms which once on Britons blazed,
When, flushed with conquest, to the charge they came,
That power repelled, and *Freedom's* fabrick raised,
She leaves her soldier—*famine* and a *name!*

PHILLIS WHEATLEY

c. 1753-1784

On Being Brought from Africa to America

'Twas mercy brought me from my *Pagan* land,
Taught my benighted soul to understand
That there's a God, that there's a *Saviour* too;
Once I redemption neither sought nor knew,
Some view our sable race with scornful eye,
"Their color is a diabolic die."
Remember, *Christians, Negroes,* black as *Cain,*
May be refined, and join th' angelic train.

To the University of Cambridge
in New England

While an intrinsic ardor prompts to write,
The muses promise to assist my pen;
'Twas not long since I left my native shore
The land of errors, and *Egyptian* gloom:
Father of mercy, 'twas thy gracious hand
Brought me in safety from those dark abodes.
    Students, to you 'tis giv'n to scan the heights
Above, to traverse the ethereal space,
And mark the systems of revolving worlds.
Still more, ye sons of science, ye receive
The blissful news by messengers from heav'n
How *Jesus'* blood for your redemption flows.
See Him with hands outstretched upon the cross;
Immense compassion in His bosom glows;
He hears revilers, nor resents their scorn;
What matchless mercy in the Son of God!
When the whole human race by sin had fall'n,

He deign'd to die that they might rise again,
And share with Him in the sublimest skies,
Life without death, and glory without end.
   Improve your privileges while they stay,
Ye pupils, and each hour redeem, that bears
Or good or bad report of you to heav'n.
Let sin, that baneful evil to the soul,
By you be shunned, nor once remit your guard;
Suppress the deadly serpent in its egg.
Ye blooming plants of human race divine,
An *Ethiop* tells you 'tis your greatest foe;
Its transient sweetness turns to endless pain,
And in immense perdition sinks the soul.

An Hymn to the Morning

Attend my lays, ye ever honour'd nine,
Assist my labours, and my strains refine;
In smoothest numbers pour the notes along,
For bright *Aurora* now demands my song.
   Aurora hail, and all the thousand dyes,
Which deck thy progress through the vaulted skies;
The morn awakes, and wide extends her rays,
On ev'ry leaf the gentle zephyr plays;
Harmonious lays the feather'd race resume,
Dart the bright eye, and shake the painted plume.
   Ye shady groves, your verdant gloom display
To shield your poet from the burning day:
Calliope awake the sacred lyre,
While thy fair sisters fan the pleasing fire:
The bow'rs, the gales, the variegated skies
In all their pleasures in my bosom rise.

See in the east th' illustrious king of day!
His rising radiance drives the shades away—
But oh! I feel his fervid beams too strong,
And scarce begun, concludes th' abortive song.

To S. M., a Young African Painter, On Seeing His Works

To show the lab'ring bosom's deep intent,
And thought in living characters to paint,
When first thy pencil did those beauties give,
And breathing figures learnt from thee to live,
How did those prospects give my soul delight,
A new creation rushing on my sight?
Still, wond'rous youth! each noble path pursue,
On deathless glories fix thine ardent view:
Still may the painter's and the poet's fire
To aid thy pencil, and thy verse conspire!
And may the charms of each seraphic theme
Conduct thy footsteps to immortal fame!
High to the blissful wonders of the skies
Elate thy soul, and raise thy wishful eyes.
Thrice happy, when exalted to survey
That splendid city, crown'd with endless day,
Whose twice six gates on radiant hinges ring:
Celestial *Salem* blooms in endless spring.
  Calm and serene thy moments glide along,
And may the muse inspire each future song!
Still, with the sweets of contemplation bless'd,
May peace with balmy winds your soul invest!
But when these shades of time are chas'd away,
And darkness ends in everlasting day,

On what seraphic pinions shall we move,
And view the landscapes in the realms above?
There shall thy tongue in heav'nly murmurs flow,
And there my muse with heav'nly transport glow:
No more to tell of *Damon's* tender sighs,
Or rising radiance of *Aurora's* eyes,
For nobler themes demand a nobler strain,
And purer language on th' ethereal plain.
Cease, gentle muse! the solemn gloom of night
Now seals the fair creation from my sight.

JOHN QUINCY ADAMS
1767-1848

The Wants of Man

"Man wants but little here below,
Nor wants that little long."
—GOLDSMITH'S HERMIT

I.

"Man wants but little here below,
   Nor wants that little long."
'Tis not with ME exactly so,
   But 'tis so in the song.
MY wants are many, and if told
   Would muster many a score;
And were each wish a mint of gold,
   I still should long for more.

II.

What first I want is daily bread,
   And canvas backs and wine;
And all the realms of nature spread
   Before me when I dine.
Four courses scarcely can provide
   My appetite to quell,
With four choice cooks from France, beside,
   To dress my dinner well.

III.

What next I want, at heavy cost,
   Is elegant attire;—
Black sable furs, for winter's frost,
   And silks for summer's fire,

And Cashmere shawls, and Brussels lace
    My bosom's front to deck,
And diamond rings my hands to grace,
    And rubies for my neck.

IV.

And then I want a mansion fair,
    A dwelling house, in style,
Four stories high, for wholesome air—
    A massive marble pile;
With halls for banquets and balls,
    All furnished rich and fine;
With stabled studs in fifty stalls,
    And cellars for my wine.

V.

I want a garden and a park,
    My dwelling to surround—
A thousand acres (bless the mark),
    With walls encompassed round—
Where flocks may range and herds may low,
    And kids and lambkins play,
And flowers and fruits commingled grow,
    All Eden to display.

VI.

I want, when summer's foliage falls,
    And autumn strips the trees,
A house within the city's walls,
    For comfort and for ease.

But here, as space is somewhat scant,
  And acres somewhat rare,
My house in town I only want
  To occupy—a square.

VII.

I want a steward, butler, cooks;
  A coachman, footman, grooms,
A library of well-bound books,
  And picture-garnished rooms;
Corregios, Magdalen, and Night,
  The matron of the chair;
Guido's fleet coursers in their flight,
  And Claudes at least a pair.

VIII.

I want a cabinet profuse
  Of medals, coins, and gems;
A printing press, for private use,
  Of fifty thousand EMS;
And plants, and minerals, and shells;
  Worms, insects, fishes, birds;
And every beast on earth that dwells,
  In solitude or herds.

IX.

I want a board of burnished plate,
  Of silver and of gold;
Tureens of twenty pounds in weight,
  With sculpture's richest mould;

Plateaus, with chandeliers and lamps,
    Plates, dishes—all the same;
And porcelain vases, with the stamps
    Of Sevres, Angouleme.

X.

And maples, of fair glossy stain,
    Must form my chamber doors,
And carpets of the Wilton grain
    Must cover all my floors;
My walls, with tapestry bedeck'd,
    Must never be outdone;
And damask curtains must protect
    Their colors from the sun.

XI.

And mirrors of the largest pane
    From Venice must be brought;
And sandal-wood, and bamboo cane,
    For chairs and tables bought;
On all the mantel-pieces, clocks
    Of thrice-gilt bronze must stand,
And screens of ebony and box
    Invite the stranger's hand.

XII.

I want (who does not want?) a wife,
    Affectionate and fair,
To solace all the woes of life,
    And all its joys to share;

Of temper sweet, of yielding will,
 Of firm, yet placid mind,
With all my faults to love me still,
 With sentiment refin'd.

XIII.

And as Time's car incessant runs,
 And Fortune fills my store,
I want of daughters and of sons
 From eight to half a score.
I want (alas! can mortal dare
 Such bliss on earth to crave?)
That all the girls be chaste and fair—
 The boys all wise and brave.

XIV.

And when my bosom's darling sings,
 With melody divine,
A pedal harp of many strings
 Must with her voice combine.
A piano, exquisitely wrought,
 Must open stand, apart,
That all my daughters may be taught
 To win the stranger's heart.

XV.

My wife and daughters will desire
 Refreshment from perfumes,
Cosmetics for the skin require,
 And artificial blooms.

The civit fragrance shall dispense,
 And treasur'd sweets return;
Cologne revive the flagging sense,
 And smoking amber burn.

XVI.

And when at night my weary head
 Begins to droop and dose,
A southern chamber holds my bed,
 For nature's soft repose;
With blankets, counterpanes, and sheet,
 Mattrass, and bed of down,
And comfortables for my feet,
 And pillows for my crown.

XVII.

I want a warm and faithful friend,
 To cheer the adverse hour,
Who ne'er to flatter will descend,
 Nor bend the knee to power;
A friend to chide me when I'm wrong,
 My inmost soul to see;
And that my friendship prove as strong
 For him, as his for me.

XVIII.

I want a kind and tender heart,
 For others wants to feel;
A soul secure from Fortune's dart,
 And bosom arm'd with steel;

To bear divine chastisement's rod.
  And mingling in my plan,
Submission to the will of God,
  With charity to man.

XIX.

I want a keen, observing eye,
  An ever-listening ear,
The truth through all disguise to spy,
  And wisdom's voice to hear;
A tongue, to speak at virtue's need,
  In Heaven's sublimest strain;
And lips, the cause of man to plead,
  And never plead in vain.

XX.

I want uninterrupted health,
  Throughout my long career,
And streams of never-failing wealth,
  To scatter far and near;
The destitute to clothe and feed,
  Free bounty to bestow;
Supply the helpless orphan's need,
  And soothe the widow's woe.

XXI.

I want the genius to conceive,
  The talents to unfold,
Designs, the vicious to retrieve,
  The virtuous to uphold;

Inventive power, combining skill,
    A persevering soul,
Of human hearts to mould the will,
    And reach from pole to pole.

XXII.

I want the seals of power and place,
    The ensigns of command,
Charged by the people's unbought grace,
    To rule my native land.
Nor crown, nor sceptre would I ask
    But from my country's will,
By day, by night, to ply the task
    Her cup of bliss to fill.

XXIII.

I want the voice of honest praise
    To follow me behind,
And to be thought in future days
    The friend of human kind;
That after ages, as they rise,
    Exulting may proclaim,
In choral union to the skies,
    Their blessings on my name.

XXIV.

These are the wants of mortal man;
    I cannot want them long,
For life itself is but a span,
    And earthly bliss a song.

My last great want, absorbing all,
   Is, when beneath the sod,
And summon'd to my final call,
   The mercy of my God.

XXV.

And oh! while circles in my veins
   Of life the purple stream,
And yet a fragment small remains
   Of nature's transient dream,
My soul, in humble hope unscar'd,
   Forget not thou to pray,
That this thy WANT may be prepared
   To meet the Judgment Day.

FRANCIS SCOTT KEY

1779-1843

Defence of Fort McHenry

O! say can you see, by the dawn's early light,
What so proudly we hail'd at the twilight's last gleaming,
Whose broad stripes and bright stars through the perilous fight,
O'er the ramparts we watch'd, were so gallantly streaming?
And the rockets' red glare, the bombs bursting in air,
Gave proof through the night that our flag was still there—
O! say, does that star-spangled banner yet wave
O'er the land of the free, and the home of the brave?

On the shore, dimly seen through the mists of the deep,
Where the foe's haughty host in dread silence reposes,
What is that which the breeze o'er the towering steep,
As it fitfully blows, half conceals, half discloses?
Now it catches the gleam of the morning's first beam,
In full glory reflected now shines on the stream—
'Tis the star-spangled banner, O! long may it wave
O'er the land of the free, and the home of the brave.

And where is that band who so vauntingly swore
That the havock of war and the battle's confusion
A home and a country should leave us no more?
Their blood has wash'd out their foul foot-steps' pollution.
No refuge could save the hireling and slave,
From the terror of flight or the gloom of the grave,
And the star-spangled banner in triumph doth wave
O'er the land of the free, and the home of the brave.

O! thus be it ever when freemen shall stand
  Between their lov'd home, and the war's desolation,
Blest with vict'ry and peace, may the heav'n-rescued land
  Praise the power that hath made and preserv'd us a nation!
    Then conquer we must, when our cause it is just,
    And this be our motto—"In God is our trust!"
      And the star-spangled banner in triumph shall wave
      O'er the land of the free, and the home of the brave.

Washington Allston
1779-1843

Coleridge

And thou art gone most loved, most honor'd friend!
No—never more thy gentle voice shall blend
With air of earth its pure ideal tones—
Binding in one, as with harmonious zones,
The heart and intellect. And I no more
Shall with thee gaze on that unfathom'd deep,
The Human Soul; as when, push'd off the shore,
Thy mystic bark would thro' the darkness sweep—
Itself the while so bright! For oft we seem'd
As on some starless sea—all dark above,
All dark below—yet, onward as we drove,
To plough up light that ever round us stream'd
But he who mourns is not as one bereft
Of all he loved: thy living Truths are left.

On the Statue of an Angel, by Bienaimé, in the Possession of J. S. Copley Greene, Esq.

Ah, who can look on that celestial face,
And kindred for it claim with aught on earth?
If ever here more lovely form had birth,—
No, never that supernal purity,—that grace
So eloquent of unimpassioned love!
That, by a simple movement, thus imparts
Its own harmonious peace, the while our hearts
Rise, as by instinct, to the world above.
And yet we look on cold, unconscious stone.

But what is *that* which thus our spirits own
As Truth and Life? 'T is not material Art,—
But e'en the Sculptor's soul to sense unsealed.
O, never may he doubt,—its witness so revealed,—
There lives within him an immortal part!

Samuel Woodworth
1785-1842

The Bucket

Air—The Flower of Dumblane

How dear to this heart are the scenes of my childhood,
    When fond recollection presents them to view!
The orchard, the meadow, the deep-tangled wild-wood,
    And every loved spot which my infancy knew!
The wide-spreading pond, and the mill that stood by it,
    The bridge, and the rock where the cataract fell,
The cot of my father, the dairy-house nigh it,
    And e'en the rude bucket that hung in the well—
The old oaken bucket, the iron-bound bucket,
The moss-covered bucket which hung in the well.

That moss-covered vessel I hail'd as a treasure,
    For often at noon, when return'd from the field,
I found it the source of an exquisite pleasure,
    The purest and sweetest that nature can yield.
How ardent I seized it, with hands that were glowing,
    And quick to the white-pebbled bottom it fell;
Then soon, with the emblem of truth overflowing,
    And dripping with coolness, it rose from the well—
The old oaken bucket, the iron-bound bucket,
The moss-covered bucket, arose from the well.

How sweet from the green mossy brim to receive it,
   As poised on the curb it inclined to my lips!
Not a full blushing goblet could tempt me to leave it.
   The brightest that beauty or revelry sips.
And now, far removed from the loved habitation,
   The tear of regret will intrusively swell.
As fancy reverts to my father's plantation.
   And sighs for the bucket that hangs in the well—
The old oaken bucket, the iron-bound bucket,
The moss-covered bucket that hangs in the well!

John Howard Payne
1791-1852

Home, Sweet Home!

'Mid pleasures and palaces though we may roam,
Be it ever so humble, there's *no* place like home.
A charm from the sky seems to hallow us there,
Which, seek through the *world,* is ne'er met with elsewhere.
    Home! sweet home!
    There's no place like home!

An exile from home, splendour dazzles in vain!
Oh! give me my lowly thatch'd cottage again!
The birds singing gaily that came at my call,
Give me *them,* with the *peace of mind* DEARER than all!
    Home! sweet home!
    There's no place like home!

LYDIA HUNTLEY SIGOURNEY
1791-1865

Indian Names

*"How can the red men be forgotten, while so many of our states
and territories, bays, lakes and rivers, are indelibly stamped by
names of their giving?"*

Ye say they all have passed away,
   That noble race and brave,
That their light canoes have vanished
   From off the crested wave;
That 'mid the forests where they roamed
   There rings no hunter shout,
But their names is on your waters,
   Ye may not wash it out.

'Tis where Ontario's billow
   Like Ocean's surge is curled,
Where strong Niagara's thunders wake
   The echo of the world.
Where red Missouri bringeth
   Rich tribute from the west,
And Rappahannock sweetly sleeps
   On green Virginia's breast.

Ye say their cone-like cabins,
   That clustered o'er the vale,
Have fled away like withered leaves
   Before the autumn gale,
But their memory liveth on your hills,
   Their baptism on your shore,
Your everlasting rivers speak
   Their dialect of yore.

Old Massachusetts wears it,
    Within her lordly crown,
And broad Ohio bears it,
    Amid his young renown;
Connecticut hath wreathed it
    Where her quiet foliage waves,
And bold Kentucky breathed it hoarse
    Through all her ancient caves.

Wachuset hides its lingering voice
    Within his rocky heart,
And Alleghany graves its tone
    Throughout his lofty chart;
Monadnock on his forehead hoar
    Doth seal the sacred trust,
Your mountains build their monument,
    Though ye destroy their dust.

Ye call these red-browed brethren
    The insects of an hour,
Crushed like the noteless worm amid
    The regions of their power;
Ye drive them from their father's lands,
    Ye break of faith the seal,
But can ye from the court of Heaven
    Exclude their last appeal?

Ye see their unresisting tribes,
    With toilsome step and slow,
On through the trackless desert pass,
    A caravan of woe;
Think ye the Eternal's ear is deaf?
    His sleepless vision dim?
Think ye the *soul's blood* may not cry
    From that far land to him?

To the First Slave Ship

First of that train which cursed the wave,
　　And from the rifled cabin bore,
Inheritor of wo,—*the slave*
　　To bless his palm-tree's shade no more.

Dire engine!—o'er the troubled main
　　Borne on in unresisted state,—
Know'st thou within thy dark domain
　　The secrets of thy prison'd freight?—

Hear'st thou *their* moans whom hope hath fled?—
　　Wild cries, in agonizing starts?—
Know'st thou thy humid sails are spread
　　With ceaseless sighs from broken hearts?—

The fetter'd chieftain's burning tear,—
　　The parted lover's mute despair,—
The childless mother's pang severe,—
　　The orphan's misery, are there.

Ah!—could'st thou from the scroll of fate
　　The annal read of future years,
Stripes,—tortures,—unrelenting hate.
　　And death-gasps drown'd in slavery's tears.

Down,—down,—beneath the cleaving main
　　Thou fain would'st plunge where monsters lie,
Rather than ope the gates of pain
　　For time and for Eternity.—

Oh Afric!—what has been thy crime?—
　　That thus like Eden's fratricide,
A mark is set upon thy clime,
　　And every brother shuns thy side.—

Yet are thy wrongs, thou long-distrest!—
    Thy burdens, by the world unweigh'd,
Safe in that *Unforgetful Breast*
    Where all the sins of earth are laid.—

Poor outcast slave!—Our guilty land
    Should tremble while she drinks thy tears,
Or sees in vengeful silence stand,
    The beacon of thy shorten'd years;—

Should shrink to hear her sons proclaim
    The sacred truth that heaven is just,—
Shrink even at her Judge's name,—
    "Jehovah,—Saviour of the opprest."

The Sun upon thy forehead frown'd,
    But Man more cruel far than he,
Dark fetters on thy spirit bound:—
    Look to the mansions of the free!

Look to that realm where chains unbind,—
    Where the pale tyrant drops his rod,
And where the patient sufferers find
    A friend,—a father in their God.

WILLIAM CULLEN BRYANT
1794-1878

Thanatopsis

To him who in the love of Nature holds
Communion with her visible forms, she speaks
A various language; for his gayer hours
She has a voice of gladness, and a smile
And eloquence of beauty, and she glides
Into his darker musings, with a mild
And healing sympathy, that steals away
Their sharpness, ere he is aware. When thoughts
Of the last bitter hour come like a blight
Over thy spirit, and sad images
Of the stern agony, and shroud, and pall,
And breathless darkness, and the narrow house,
Make thee to shudder and grow sick at heart;—
Go forth, under the open sky, and list
To Nature's teachings, while from all around—
Earth and her waters, and the depths of air—
Comes a still voice;—

              Yet a few days, and thee
The all-beholding sun shall see no more
In all his course; nor yet in the cold ground,
Where thy pale form was laid with many tears,
Nor in the embrace of ocean, shall exist
Thy image. Earth, that nourished thee, shall claim
Thy growth, to be resolved to earth again,
And, lost each human trace, surrendering up
Thine individual being, shalt thou go
To mix forever with the elements,
To be a brother to the insensible rock

And to the sluggish clod, which the rude swain
Turns with his share, and treads upon. The oak
Shall send his roots abroad, and pierce thy mould.

  Yet not to thine eternal resting-place
Shalt thou retire alone, nor couldst thou wish
Couch more magnificent. Thou shalt lie down
With patriarchs of the infant world—with kings,
The powerful of the earth—the wise, the good,
Fair forms, and hoary seers of ages past,
All in one mighty sepulchre. The hills
Rock-ribbed and ancient as the sun,—the vales
Stretching in pensive quietness between;
The venerable woods—rivers that move
In majesty, and the complaining brooks
That make the meadows green; and, poured round all,
Old Ocean's gray and melancholy waste,—
Are but the solemn decorations all
Of the great tomb of man. The golden sun,
The planets, all the infinite host of heaven,
Are shining on the sad abodes of death
Through the still lapse of ages. All that tread
The globe are but a handful to the tribes
That slumber in its bosom.—Take the wings
Of morning, pierce the Barcan wilderness,
Or lose thyself in the continuous woods
Where rolls the Oregon, and hears no sound,
Save his own dashings—yet the dead are there;
And millions in those solitudes, since first
The flight of years began, have laid them down
In their last sleep—the dead reign there alone.
So shalt thou rest, and what if thou withdraw
In silence from the living, and no friend

Take note of thy departure? All that breathe
Will share thy destiny. The gay will laugh
When thou art gone, the solemn brood of care
Plod on, and each one as before will chase
His favorite phantom; yet all these shall leave
Their mirth and their employments, and shall come
And make their bed with thee. As the long train
Of ages glides away, the sons of men—
The youth in life's fresh spring, and he who goes
In the full strength of years, matron and maid,
The speechless babe, and the gray-headed man—
Shall one by one be gathered to thy side,
By those, who in their turn shall follow them.

    So live, that when thy summons comes to join
The innumerable caravan, which moves
To that mysterious realm, where each shall take
His chamber in the silent halls of death,
Thou go not, like the quarry-slave at night,
Scourged to his dungeon, but, sustained and soothed
By an unfaltering trust, approach thy grave
Like one who wraps the drapery of his couch
About him, and lies down to pleasant dreams.

Summer Wind

    It is a sultry day; the sun has drank
The dew that lay upon the morning grass,
There is no rustling in the lofty elm
That canopies my dwelling, and its shade
Scarce cools me. All is silent, save the faint
And interrupted murmur of the bee,
Settling on the sick flowers, and then again

Instantly on the wing. The plants around
Feel the too potent fervors; the tall maize
Rolls up its long green leaves; the clover droops
Its tender foliage, and declines its blooms.
But far in the fierce sunshine tower the hills,
With all their growth of woods, silent and stern,
As if the scorching heat and dazzling light
Were but an element they loved. Bright clouds,
Motionless pillars of the brazen heaven;—
Their bases on the mountains—their white tops
Shining in the far ether—fire the air
With a reflected radiance, and make turn
The gazer's eye away. For me, I lie
Languidly in the shade, where the thick turf,
Yet virgin from the kisses of the sun,
Retains some freshness, and I woo the wind
That still delays its coming. Why so slow,
Gentle and voluble spirit of the air?
Oh, come and breathe upon the fainting earth
Coolness and life. Is it that in his caves
He hears me? See, on yonder woody ridge,
The pine is bending his proud top, and now,
Among the nearer groves, chestnut and oak
Are tossing their green boughs about. He comes!
Lo, where the grassy meadow runs in waves!
The deep distressful silence of the scene
Breaks up with mingling of unnumbered sounds
And universal motion. He is come,
Shaking a shower of blossoms from the shrubs,
And bearing on their fragrance; and he brings
Music of birds, and rustling of young boughs,
And sound of swaying branches, and the voice
Of distant waterfalls. All the green herbs

Are stirring in his breath; a thousand flowers,
By the road-side and the borders of the brook,
Nod gaily to each other; glossy leaves
Are twinkling in the sun, as if the dew
Were on them yet, and silver waters break
Into small waves and sparkle as he comes.

Autumn Woods

   Ere, in the northern gale,
The summer tresses of the trees are gone,
The woods of Autumn, all around our vale,
   Have put their glory on.

   The mountains that infold
In their wide sweep, the colored landscape round,
Seem groups of giant kings, in purple and gold,
   That guard the enchanted ground.

   I roam the woods that crown
The upland, where the mingled splendors glow,
Where the gay company of trees look down
   On the green fields below.

   My steps are not alone
In these bright walks; the sweet southwest, at play,
Flies, rustling, where the painted leaves are strown
   Along the winding way.

   And far in heaven, the while,
The sun, that sends that gale to wander here,
Pours out on the fair earth his quiet smile,—
   The sweetest of the year.

Where now the solemn shade,
Verdure and gloom where many branches meet;
So grateful, when the noon of summer made
    The valleys sick with heat?

Let in through all the trees
Come the strange rays; the forest depths are bright;
Their sunny-colored foliage, in the breeze,
    Twinkles, like beams of light.

The rivulet, late unseen,
Where bickering through the shrubs its waters run,
Shines with the image of its golden screen,
    And glimmerings of the sun.

But 'neath yon crimson tree,
Lover to listening maid might breathe his flame,
Nor mark, within its roseate canopy,
    Her blush of maiden shame.

Oh, Autumn! why so soon
Depart the hues that make thy forests glad;
Thy gentle wind and thy fair sunny noon,
    And leave thee wild and sad!

Ah! 'twere a lot too blest
Forever in thy colored shades to stray;
Amidst the kisses of the soft southwest
    To rove and dream for aye;

And leave the vain low strife
That makes men mad—the tug for wealth and power,
The passions and the cares that wither life,
    And waste its little hour.

To a Waterfowl

Whither, midst falling dew,
While glow the heavens with the last steps of day,
Far, through their rosy depths, dost thou pursue
Thy solitary way?

Vainly the fowler's eye
Might mark thy distant flight to do thee wrong,
As, darkly painted on the crimson sky,
Thy figure floats along.

Seek'st thou the plashy brink
Of weedy lake, or marge of river wide,
Or where the rocking billows rise and sink
On the chafed ocean-side?

There is a Power whose care
Teaches thy way along that pathless coast—
The desert and illimitable air—
Lone wandering, but not lost.

All day thy wings have fanned,
At that far height, the cold, thin atmosphere,
Yet stoop not, weary, to the welcome land,
Though the dark night is near.

And soon that toil shall end;
Soon shalt thou find a summer home, and rest,
And scream among thy fellows; reeds shall bend,
Soon, o'er thy sheltered nest.

Thou'rt gone, the abyss of heaven
Hath swallowed up thy form; yet, on my heart
Deeply has sunk the lesson thou hast given,
And shall not soon depart.

He who, from zone to zone,
Guides through the boundless sky thy certain flight,
In the long way that I must tread alone,
Will lead my steps aright.

Sonnet—to an American Painter Departing for Europe

Thine eyes shall see the light of distant skies:
   Yet, Cole! thy heart shall bear to Europe's strand
   A living image of thy native land,
Such as on thy own glorious canvass lies.
Lone lakes—savannahs where the bison roves—
   Rocks rich with summer garlands—solemn streams—
   Skies, where the desert eagle wheels and screams—
Spring bloom and autumn blaze of boundless groves.
Fair scenes shall greet thee where thou goest—fair,
   But different—every where the trace of men,
   Paths, homes, graves, ruins, from the lowest glen
To where life shrinks from the fierce Alpine air.
   Gaze on them, till the tears shall dim thy sight,
   But keep that earlier, wilder image bright.

Abraham Lincoln

Oh, slow to smite and swift to spare,
   Gentle and merciful and just!
Who, in the fear of God, didst bear
   The sword of power, a nation's trust!

In sorrow by thy bier we stand,
  Amid the awe that hushes all,
And speak the anguish of a land
  That shook with horror at thy fall.

Thy task is done; the bond are free;
  We bear thee to an honored grave,
Whose proudest monument shall be
  The broken fetters of the slave.

Pure was thy life; its bloody close
  Hath placed thee with the sons of light,
Among the noble host of those
  Who perished in the cause of Right.

November

Yet one smile more, departing distant sun!
  One mellow smile through the soft vapory air,
Ere, o'er the frozen earth, the loud winds run,
  Or snows are sifted o'er the meadows bare.
One smile on the brown hills and naked trees,
  And the dark rocks whose summer wreaths are cast,
And the blue Gentian flower, that, in the breeze,
  Nods lonely, of her beauteous race the last.
Yet a few sunny days, in which the bee
  Shall murmur by the hedge that skirts the way,
The cricket chirp upon the russet lea,
  And man delight to linger in thy ray.
Yet one rich smile, and we will try to bear
The piercing winter frost, and winds, and darkened air.

To the Fringed Gentian

Thou blossom bright with autumn dew,
And colored with the heaven's own blue,
That openest when the quiet light
Succeeds the keen and frosty night,

Thou comest not when violets lean
O'er wandering brooks and springs unseen,
Or columbines, in purple dressed,
Nod o'er the ground-bird's hidden nest.

Thou waitest late and com'st alone,
When woods are bare and birds are flown,
And frost and shortening days portend
The aged year is near his end.

Then doth thy sweet and quiet eye
Look through its fringes to the sky,
Blue—blue—as if that sky let fall
A flower from its cerulean wall.

I would that thus, when I shall see
The hour of death draw near to me,
Hope, blossoming within my heart,
May look to heaven as I depart.

An Evening Revery

The summer day is closed—the sun is set:
Well they have done their office, those bright hours,
The latest of whose train goes softly out
In the red west. The green blade of the ground
Has risen, and herds have cropped it; the young twig
Has spread its plaited tissues to the sun;

Flowers of the garden and the waste have blown
And withered; seeds have fallen upon the soil,
From bursting cells, and in their graves await
Their resurrection. Insects from the pools
Have filled the air awhile with humming wings,
That now are stilled for ever; painted moths
Have wandered the blue sky, and died again;
The mother-bird hath broken for her brood
Their prison shell, or shoved them from the nest,
Plumed for their earliest flight. In bright alcoves,
In woodland cottages with barky walls,
In noisome cells of the tumultuous town,
Mothers have clasped with joy the new-born babe.
Graves by the lonely forest, by the shore
Of rivers and of ocean, by the ways
Of the thronged city, have been hollowed out
And filled, and closed. This day hath parted friends
That ne'er before were parted; it hath knit
New friendships; it hath seen the maiden plight
Her faith, and trust her peace to him who long
Had wooed; and it hath heard, from lips which late
Were eloquent of love, the first harsh word,
That told the wedded one her peace was flown.
Farewell to the sweet sunshine! One glad day
Is added now to Childhood's merry days,
And one calm day to those of quiet Age.
Still the fleet hours run on; and as I lean,
Amid the thickening darkness, lamps are lit,
By those who watch the dead, and those who twine
Flowers for the bride. The mother from the eyes
Of her sick infant shades the painful light,
And sadly listens to his quick-drawn breath.

O thou great Movement of the Universe,
Or Change, or Flight of Time—for ye are one!
That bearest, silently, this visible scene
Into night's shadow and the streaming rays
Of starlight, whither art thou bearing me?
I feel the mighty current sweep me on,
Yet know not whither. Man foretells afar
The courses of the stars; the very hour
He knows when they shall darken or grow bright;
Yet doth the eclipse of Sorrow and of Death
Come unforewarned. Who next, of those I love,
Shall pass from life, or, sadder yet, shall fall
From virtue? Strife with foes, or bitterer strife
With friends, or shame and general scorn of men—
Which who can bear?—or the fierce rack of pain—
Lie they within my path? Or shall the years
Push me, with soft and inoffensive pace,
Into the stilly twilight of my age?
Or do the portals of another life
Even now, while I am glorying in my strength,
Impend around me? Oh! beyond that bourne,
In the vast cycle of being which begins
At that dread threshold, with what fairer forms
Shall the great law of change and progress clothe
Its workings? Gently—so have good men taught—
Gently, and without grief, the old shall glide
Into the new; the eternal flow of things,
Like a bright river of the fields of heaven,
Shall journey onward in perpetual peace.

Maria Gowen Brooks

c. 1794-1845

Composed at the Request of a Lady, and Descriptive of Her Feelings

She Returned to the North, and Died Soon After

Adieu, fair isle! I love thy bowers,
   I love thy dark-eyed daughters there;
The cool pomegranate's scarlet flowers
   Look brighter in their jetty hair.

They praised my forehead's stainless white;
   And when I thirsted, gave a draught
From the full clustering cocoa's height,
   And smiling, blessed me as I quaff'd.

Well pleased, the kind return I gave,
   And, clasped in their embraces' twine,
Felt the soft breeze, like Lethe's wave,
   Becalm this beating heart of mine.

Why will my heart so wildly beat?
   Say, Seraphs, is my lot too blest,
That thus a fitful, feverish heat
   Must rifle me of health and rest?

Alas! I fear my native snows—
   A clime too cold, a heart too warm—
Alternate chills—alternate glows—
   Too fiercely threat my flower-like form.

The orange-tree has fruit and flowers;
   The grenadilla, in its bloom,
Hangs o'er its high, luxuriant bowers,
   Like fringes from a Tyrian loom.

When the white coffee-blossoms swell,
   The fair moon full, the evening long,
I love to hear the warbling bell,
   And sun-burnt peasant's wayward song.

Drive gently on, dark muleteer,
   And the light seguidilla frame;
Fain would I listen still, to hear
   At every close thy mistress' name.

Adieu, fair isle! the waving palm
   Is pencilled on thy purest sky;
Warm sleeps the bay, the air is balm,
   And, soothed to languor, scarce a sigh

Escapes for those I love so well,
   For those I've loved and left so long,
On me their fondest musings dwell,
   To them alone my sighs belong.

On, on, my bark! blow southern breeze!
   No longer would I lingering stay;
'Twere better far *to die* with these
   Than *live in pleasure* far away.

GEORGE MOSES HORTON
c. 1798-c. 1883

On Liberty and Slavery

Alas! and am I born for this,
　　To wear this slavish chain?
Deprived of all created bliss,
　　Through hardship, toil and pain!

How long have I in bondage lain,
　　And languished to be free!
Alas! and must I still complain—
　　Deprived of liberty.

Oh, Heaven! and is there no relief
　　This side the silent grave—
To soothe the pain—to quell the grief
　　And anguish of a slave?

Come Liberty, thou cheerful sound,
　　Roll through my ravished ears!
Come, let my grief in joys be drowned,
　　And drive away my fears.

Say unto foul oppression, Cease:
　　Ye tyrants rage no more,
And let the joyful trump of peace,
　　Now bid the vassal soar.

Soar on the pinions of that dove
　　Which long has cooed for thee,
And breathed her notes from Afric's grove,
　　The sound of Liberty.

Oh, Liberty! thou golden prize,
    So often sought by blood—
We crave thy sacred sun to rise,
    The gift of nature's God!

Bid Slavery hide her haggard face,
    And barbarism fly:
I scorn to see the sad disgrace
    In which enslaved I lie.

Dear Liberty! upon thy breast,
    I languish to respire;
And like the Swan unto her nest,
    I'd to thy smiles retire.

Oh, blest asylum—heavenly balm!
    Unto thy boughs I flee—
And in thy shades the storm shall calm,
    With songs of Liberty!

GEORGE POPE MORRIS
1802-1864

The Oak

Woodman, spare that tree!
　Touch not a single bough!
In youth it sheltered me,
　And I'll protect it now.
'Twas my forefather's hand
　That placed it near his cot;
There, woodman, let it stand,
　Thy axe shall harm it not!

That old familiar tree,
　Whose glory and renown
Are spread o'er land and sea,
　And wouldst thou hack it down?
Woodman, forbear thy stroke!
　Cut not its earth-bound ties;
Oh, spare that aged oak,
　Now towering to the skies!

When but an idle boy
　I sought its grateful shade;
In all their gushing joy
　Here too my sisters played.
My mother kiss'd me here;
　My father press'd my hand—
Forgive this foolish tear,
　But let that old oak stand!

My heart-strings round thee cling,
　Close as thy bark, old friend!
Here shall the wild-bird sing,
　And still thy branches bend.
Old tree! the storm still brave!
　And, woodman, leave the spot;
While I've a hand to save,
　Thy axe shall harm it not.

LYDIA MARIA CHILD
1802-1880

The New-England Boy's Song About Thanksgiving Day

Over the river, and through the wood,
  To grandfather's house we go;
    The horse knows the way,
    To carry the sleigh,
  Through the white and drifted snow.

Over the river, and through the wood,
  To grandfather's house away!
    We would not stop
    For doll or top,
  For 'tis Thanksgiving day.

Over the river, and through the wood,
  Oh, how the wind does blow!
    In stings the toes,
    And bites the nose,
  As over the ground we go.

Over the river, and through the wood,
  With a clear blue winter sky,
    The dogs do bark,
    And children hark,
  As we go jingling by.

Over the river, and through the wood,
  To have a first-rate play—
    Hear the bells ring
    Ting a ling ding,
  Hurra for Thanksgiving day!

Over the river, and through the wood—
  No matter for winds that blow;
    Or if we get
    The sleigh upset,
  Into a bank of snow.

Over the river, and through the wood,
  To see little John and Ann;
    We will kiss them all,
    And play snow-ball,
  And stay as long as we can.

Over the river, and through the wood,
  Trot fast, my dapple grey!
    Spring over the ground,
    Like a hunting hound,
  For 't is Thanksgiving day!

Over the river, and through the wood,
  And straight through the barn-yard gate;
    We seem to go
    Extremely slow,
  It is so hard to wait.

Over the river, and through the wood—
  Old Jowler hears our bells;
    He shakes his pow,
    With a loud bow wow,
  And thus the news he tells.

Over the river, and through the wood—
  When grandmother sees us come,
    She will say, Oh dear,
    The children are here,
  Bring a pie for every one.

Over the river, and through the wood—
   Now grandmother's cap I spy!
     Hurra for the fun!
     Is the pudding done?
   Hurra for the pumpkin pie!

RALPH WALDO EMERSON
1803–1882

Concord Hymn

Sung at the completion of the Battle Monument, July 4, 1837

By the rude bridge that arched the flood,
　　Their flag to April's breeze unfurled,
Here once the embattled farmers stood
　　And fired the shot heard round the world.

The foe long since in silence slept;
　　Alike the conqueror silent sleeps;
And Time the ruined bridge has swept
　　Down the dark stream which seaward creeps.

On this green bank, by this soft stream,
　　We set today a votive stone;
That memory may their deed redeem,
　　When, like our sires, our sons are gone.

Spirit, that made those heroes dare,
　　To die, and leave their children free,
Bid Time and Nature gently spare
　　The shaft we raise to them and thee.

Dirge

Knows he who tills this lonely field
　　To reap its scanty corn,
What mystic fruit his acres yield
　　At midnight and at morn?

In the long sunny afternoon
　　The plain was full of ghosts;
I wandered up, I wandered down,
　　Beset by pensive hosts.

The winding Concord gleamed below,
   Pouring as wide a flood
As when my brothers, long ago,
   Came with me to the wood.

But they are gone,—the holy ones
   Who trod with me this lovely vale;
The strong, star-bright companions
   Are silent, low and pale.

My good, my noble, in their prime,
   Who made this world the feast it was,
Who learned with me the lore of time,
   Who loved this dwelling-place!

The Rhodora

On Being Asked, Whence Is the Flower?

In May, when sea winds pierced our solitudes,
I found the fresh rhodora in the woods,
Spreading its leafless blooms in a damp nook,
To please the desert and the sluggish brook.
The purple petals, fallen in the pool,
Made the black water with their beauty gay;
Here might the redbird come his plumes to cool,
And court the flower that cheapens his array.
Rhodora! if the sages ask thee why
This charm is wasted on the earth and sky,
Tell them, dear, that if eyes were made for seeing,
Then Beauty is its own excuse for being:
Why thou wert there, O rival of the rose!
I never thought to ask, I never knew:
But, in my simple ignorance, suppose
The selfsame Power that brought me there brought you.

The Snow-Storm

Announced by all the trumpets of the sky,
Arrives the snow, and, driving o'er the fields,
Seems nowhere to alight: the whited air
Hides hills and woods, the river, and the heaven,
And veils the farm-house at the garden's end.
The sled and traveller stopped, the courier's feet
Delayed, all friends shut out, the housemates sit
Around the radiant fireplace, enclosed
In a tumultuous privacy of storm.

Come see the north wind's masonry.
Out of an unseen quarry evermore
Furnished with tile, the fierce artificer
Curves his white bastions with projected roof
Round every windward stake, or tree, or door.
Speeding, the myriad-handed, his wild work
So fanciful, so savage, nought cares he
For number or proportion. Mockingly,
On coop or kennel he hangs Parian wreaths;
A swan-like form invests the hidden thorn;
Fills up the farmer's lane from wall to wall,
Maugre the farmer's sighs; and, at the gate,
A tapering turret overtops the work.
And when his hours are numbered, and the world
Is all his own, retiring, as he were not,
Leaves, when the sun appears, astonished Art
To mimic in slow structures, stone by stone,
Built in an age, the mad wind's night-work,
The frolic architecture of the snow.

Sea-Shore

I heard or seemed to hear the chiding Sea
Say, Pilgrim, why so late and slow to come?
Am I not always here, thy summer home?
Is not my voice thy music, morn and eve?
My breath thy healthful climate in the heats,
My touch thy antidote, my bay thy bath?
Was ever building like my terraces?
Was ever couch magnificent as mine?
Lie on the warm rock-ledges, and there learn
A little hut suffices like a town.
I make your sculptured architecture vain,
Vain beside mine. I drive my wedges home,
And carve the coastwise mountain into caves.
Lo! here is Rome, and Nineveh, and Thebes,
Karnak, and Pyramid, and Giant's Stairs,
Half piled or prostrate; and my newest slab
Older than all thy race.
                    Behold the Sea,
The opaline, the plentiful and strong,
Yet beautiful as is the rose in June,
Fresh as the trickling rainbow of July;
Sea full of food, the nourisher of kinds,
Purger of earth, and medicine of men;
Creating a sweet climate by my breath,
Washing out harms and griefs from memory,
And, in my mathematic ebb and flow,
Giving a hint of that which changes not.
Rich are the sea-gods:—who gives gifts but they?
They grope the sea for pearls, but more than pearls:
They pluck Force thence, and give it to the wise.

For every wave is wealth to Dædalus,
Wealth to the cunning artist who can work
This matchless strength. Where shall he find, O waves!
A load your Atlas shoulders cannot lift?

   I with my hammer pounding evermore
The rocky coast, smite Andes into dust,
Strewing my bed, and, in another age,
Rebuild a continent of better men.
Then I unbar the doors: my paths lead out
The exodus of nations: I disperse
Men to all shores that front the hoary main.

   I too have arts and sorceries;
Illusion dwells forever with the wave.
I know what spells are laid. Leave me to deal
With credulous and imaginative man;
For, though he scoop my water in his palm
A few rods off he deems it gems and clouds.
Planting strange fruits and sunshine on the shore,
I make some coast alluring, some lone isle,
To distant men, who must go there, or die.

Hamatreya

Minott, Lee, Willard, Hosmer, Meriam, Flint
Possessed the land which rendered to their toil
Hay, corn, roots, hemp, flax, apples, wool, and wood.
Each of these landlords walked amidst his farm,
Saying, ' 'Tis mine, my children's, and my name's:
How sweet the west wind sounds in my own trees!
How graceful climb those shadows on my hill!
I fancy these pure waters and the flags

Know me, as does my dog: we sympathize;
And, I affirm, my actions smack of the soil.'
Where are these men? Asleep beneath their grounds;
And strangers, fond as they, their furrows plough.
Earth laughs in flowers, to see her boastful boys
Earth-proud, proud of the earth which is not theirs;
Who steer the plough, but cannot steer their feet
Clear of the grave.
They added ridge to valley, brook to pond,
And sighed for all that bounded their domain.
'This suits me for a pasture; that's my park;
We must have clay, lime, gravel, granite-ledge,
And misty lowland, where to go for peat.
The land is well,—lies fairly to the south.
'Tis good, when you have crossed the sea and back,
To find the sitfast acres where you left them.'
Ah! the hot owner sees not Death, who adds
Him to his land, a lump of mould the more.
Hear what the Earth says:—

Earth-Song

'Mine and yours;
Mine, not yours.
Earth endures;
Stars abide—
Shine down in the old sea;
Old are the shores;
But where are old men?
I who have seen much,
Such have I never seen.

'The lawyer's deed
Ran sure,
In tail,
To them, and to their heirs
Who shall succeed,
Without fail,
Forevermore.

'Here is the land,
Shaggy with wood,
With its old valley,
Mound, and flood.
But the heritors?
Fled like the flood's foam,—
The lawyer, and the laws,
And the kingdom,
Clean swept herefrom.

'They called me theirs,
Who so controlled me;
Yet every one
Wished to stay, and is gone.
How am I theirs,
If they cannot hold me,
But I hold them?'

When I heard the Earth-song,
I was no longer brave;
My avarice cooled
Like lust in the chill of the grave.

Days

Damsels of Time, the hypocritic Days,
Muffled and dumb like barefoot dervishes,
And marching single in an endless file,
Bring diadems and fagots in their hands.
To each they offer gifts after his will,
Bread, kingdoms, stars, and sky that holds them all.
I, in my pleached garden, watched the pomp,
Forgot my morning wishes, hastily
Took a few herbs and apples, and the Day
Turned and departed silent. I too late,
Under her solemn fillet saw the scorn.

Compensation

Why should I keep holiday
    When other men have none?
Why but because, when these are gay,
    I sit and mourn alone?

And why, when mirth unseals all tongues,
    Should mine alone be dumb?
Ah! late I spoke to silent throngs,
    And now their hour is come.

The Past

The debt is paid,
The verdict said,
The Furies laid,
The plague is stayed,
All fortunes made;
Turn the key and bolt the door,
Sweet is death forevermore.
Nor haughty hope, nor swart chagrin,
Nor murdering hate, can enter in.
All is now secure and fast;
Not the gods can shake the past;
Flies-to the adamantine door
Bolted down forevermore.
None can re-enter there—
No thief so politic,
No Satan with a royal trick
Steal in by window, chink, or hole,
To bind or unbind, add what lacked,
Insert a leaf, or forge a name,
New-face or finish what is packed,
Alter or mend eternal fact.

Eros

The sense of the world is short,—
Long and various the report,—
    To love and be beloved;
Men and gods have not outlearned it;
And, how oft soe'er they've turned it,
    'Tis not to be improved.

Thine Eyes Still Shined

Thine eyes still shined for me, though far
    I lonely roved the land or sea:
As I behold yon evening star,
    Which yet beholds not me.

This morn I climbed the misty hill
    And roamed the pastures through;
How danced thy form before my path
    Amidst the deep-eyed dew!

When the redbird spread his sable wing,
    And showed his side of flame;
When the rosebud ripened to the rose,
    In both I read thy name.

Forbearance

Hast thou named all the birds without a gun?
Loved the wood rose, and left it on its stalk?
At rich men's tables eaten bread and pulse?
Unarmed, faced danger with a heart of trust?
And loved so well a high behavior,
In man or maid, that thou from speech refrained,
Nobility more nobly to repay?
O, be my friend, and teach me to be thine!

Give All to Love

Give all to love;
Obey thy heart;
Friends, kindred, days,
Estate, good-fame,
Plans, credit, and the Muse,—
Nothing refuse.

'Tis a brave master;
Let it have scope:
Follow it utterly,
Hope beyond hope:
High and more high
It dives into noon,
With wing unspent,
Untold intent;
But it is a god,
Knows its own path,
And the outlets of the sky.

It was not for the mean;
It requireth courage stout,
Souls above doubt,
Valour unbending;
Such 'twill reward,—
They shall return
More than they were,
And ever ascending.

Leave all for love;
Yet, hear me, yet,
One word more thy heart behoved,
One pulse more of firm endeavour,—

Keep thee to-day,
To-morrow, forever,
Free as an Arab
Of thy beloved.

Cling with life to the maid;
But when the surprise,
First vague shadow of surmise
Flits across her bosom young,
Of a joy apart from thee,
Free be she, fancy-free;
Nor thou detain her vesture's hem,
Nor the palest rose she flung
From her summer diadem.

Though thou loved her as thyself,
As a self of purer clay,
Though her parting dims the day,
Stealing grace from all alive;
Heartily know;
When half gods go,
The gods arrive.

SARAH HELEN WHITMAN
1803-1878

To ——

Vainly my heart had with thy sorceries striven:
It had no refuge from thy love,—no Heaven
But in thy fatal presence;—from afar
It owned thy power and trembled like a star
O'erfraught with light and splendor. Could I deem
How dark a shadow should obscure its beam?—
Could I believe that pain could ever dwell
Where thy bright presence cast its blissful spell?
Thou wert my proud palladium;—could I fear
The avenging Destinies when thou wert near?—
Thou wert my Destiny;—thy song, thy fame,
The wild enchantments clustering round thy name,
Were my soul's heritage, its royal dower;
Its glory and its kingdom and its power!

NATHANIEL HAWTHORNE
1804-1864

"I left my low and humble home"

I left my low and humble home,
Far from my Father's fields to roam.
My peaceful cot no more had charms,
My only joy was War's alarms.
I panted for the field of fight,
I gaz'd upon the deathless light,
Which o'er the Hero's grave is shed,
The glorious memory of the dead.
Ambition show'd a distant star,
That shed its radience bright and far,
And pointed to a path which led
O'er heaps of dying and of dead;
Onward I press'd with eager feet,
And War's dread thunder still would greet
My reckless ears. Where'er I trod,
I saw the green and verdant sod,
Turn red with blood of slaughter'd foes,
And Fury veil'd in smoke arose.
I gain'd the envied height, and there,
I sigh'd for that lone cottage, where
The early hours of life flew by,
On wings of youthful ecstacy.
Too late I found that Glory's ray,
Could never bring one happy day.

The Ocean

The Ocean has its silent caves,
Deep, quiet and alone;
Though there be fury on the waves,
Beneath them there is none.
The awful spirits of the deep
Hold their communion there;
And there are those for whom we weep,
The young, the bright, the fair.

Calmly the wearied seamen rest
Beneath their own blue sea.
The ocean solitudes are blest,
For there is purity.
The earth has guilt, the earth has care,
Unquiet are its graves;
But peaceful sleep is ever there,
Beneath the dark blue waves.

Henry Wadsworth Longfellow
1807-1882

From *Evangeline*

This is the forest primeval. The murmuring pines and the hemlocks,
Bearded with moss, and in garments green, indistinct in the twilight,
Stand like Druids of eld, with voices sad and prophetic,
Stand like harpers hoar, with beards that rest on their bosoms.
Loud from its rocky caverns, the deep-voiced neighboring ocean
Speaks, and in accents disconsolate answers the wail of the forest.

This is the forest primeval; but where are the hearts that beneath it
Leaped like the roe, when he hears in the woodland the voice of the
huntsman?

Where is the thatch-roofed village, the home of Acadian farmers,—
Men whose lives glided on like rivers that water the woodlands,
Darkened by shadows of earth, but reflecting an image of heaven?
Waste are those pleasant farms, and the farmers forever departed!
Scattered like dust and leaves, when the mighty blasts of October
Seize them, and whirl them aloft, and sprinkle them far o'er the ocean.
Naught but tradition remains of the beautiful village of Grand Pré.

Ye who believe in affection that hopes, and endures, and is patient,
Ye who believe in the beauty and strength of woman's devotion,
List to the mournful tradition, still sung by the pines of the forest;
List to a Tale of Love in Acadie, home of the happy.

In the Acadian land, on the shores of the Basin of Minas,
Distant, secluded, still, the little village of Grand Pré
Lay in the fruitful valley. Vast meadows stretched to the eastward,
Giving the village its name, and pasture to flocks without number.
Dikes, that the hands of the farmers had raised with labor incessant
Shut out the turbulent tides; but at stated seasons the floodgates
Opened, and welcomed the sea to wander at will o'er the meadows.

West and south there were fields of flax, and orchards and cornfields
Spreading afar and unfenced o'er the plain; and away to the northward
Blomidon rose, and the forests old, and aloft on the mountains
Sea-fogs pitched their tents, and mists from the mighty Atlantic
Looked on the happy valley, but ne'er from their station descended.
There, in the midst of its farms, reposed the Acadian village.
Strongly built were the houses, with frames of oak and of hemlock,
Such as the peasants of Normandy built in the reign of the Henries.
Thatched were the roofs, with dormer-windows; and gables projecting
Over the basement below protected and shaded the doorway.
There in the tranquil evenings of summer, when brightly the sunset
Lighted the village street, and gilded the vanes on the chimneys,
Matrons and maidens sat in snow-white caps and in kirtles
Scarlet and blue and green, with distaffs spinning the golden
Flax for the gossiping looms, whose noisy shuttles within doors
Mingled their sounds with the whir of the wheels and the songs of
    the maidens.
Solemnly down the street came the parish priest, and the children
Paused in their play to kiss the hand he extended to bless them.
Reverend walked he among them; and up rose matrons and maidens,
Hailing his slow approach with words of affectionate welcome.
Then came the laborers home from the field, and serenely the sun sank
Down to his rest, and twilight prevailed. Anon from the belfry
Softly the Angelus sounded, and over the roofs of the village
Columns of pale blue smoke, like clouds of incense ascending,
Rose from a hundred hearths, the homes of peace and contentment.
Thus dwelt together in love these simple Acadian farmers,—
Dwelt in the love of God and of man. Alike were they free from
Fear, that reigns with the tyrant, and envy, the vice of republics.
Neither locks had they to their doors, nor bars to their windows;
But their dwellings were open as day and the hearts of the owners;
There the richest was poor, and the poorest lived in abundance.

Somewhat apart from the village, and nearer the Basin of Minas,
Benedict Bellefontaine, the wealthiest farmer of Grand Pré,
Dwelt on his goodly acres; and with him, directing his household,
Gentle Evangeline lived, his child, and the pride of the village.
Stalwart and stately in form was the man of seventy winters;
Hearty and hale was he, an oak that is covered with snowflakes;
White as the snow were his locks, and his cheeks as brown as the
    oak-leaves.
Fair was she to behold, that maiden of seventeen summers.
Black were her eyes as the berry that grows on the thorn by the wayside,
Black, yet how softly they gleamed beneath the brown shade of her
    tresses!
Sweet was her breath as the breath of kine that feed in the meadows.
When in the harvest heat she bore to the reapers at noon-tide
Flagons of home-brewed ale, ah! fair in sooth was the maiden.
Fairer was she when, on Sunday morn, while the bell from its turret
Sprinkled with holy sounds the air, as the priest with his hyssop
Sprinkles the congregation, and scatters blessings upon them,
Down the long street she passed, with her chaplet of beads and her missal,
Wearing her Norman cap, and her kirtle of blue, and the ear-rings,
Brought in the olden time from France, and since, as an heirloom,
Handed down from mother to child, through long generations.
But a celestial brightness—a more ethereal beauty—
Shone on her face and encircled her form, when, after confession,
Homeward serenely she walked with God's benediction upon her.
When she had passed, it seemed like the ceasing of exquisite music.

The Sound of the Sea

The sea awoke at midnight from its sleep,
   And round the pebbly beaches far and wide
   I heard the first wave of the rising tide
   Rush onward with uninterrupted sweep;
A voice out of the silence of the deep,
   A sound mysteriously multiplied
   As of a cataract from the mountain's side,
   Or roar of winds upon a wooded steep.
So comes to us at times, from the unknown
   And inaccessible solitudes of being,
   The rushing of the sea-tides of the soul;
And inspirations, that we deem our own,
   Are some divine foreshadowing and foreseeing
   Of things beyond our reason or control.

The Arrow and The Song

I shot an arrow into the air,
It fell to earth, I knew not where;
For, so swiftly it flew, the sight
Could not follow it in its flight.

I breathed a song into the air,
It fell to earth, I knew not where;
For who has sight so keen and strong,
That it can follow the flight of song?

Long, long afterward, in an oak
I found the arrow, still unbroke;
And the song, from beginning to end,
I found again in the heart of a friend.

Aftermath

When the Summer fields are mown,
When the birds are fledged and flown,
　　And the dry leaves strew the path;
With the falling of the snow,
With the cawing of the crow,
Once again the fields we mow
　　And gather in the aftermath.

Not the sweet, new grass with flowers
Is this harvesting of ours;
　　Not the upland clover bloom;
But the rowen mixed with weeds,
Tangled tufts from marsh and meads,
Where the poppy drops its seeds
　　In the silence and the gloom.

The Children's Hour

Between the dark and the daylight,
　　When the night is beginning to lower,
Comes a pause in the day's occupations,
　　That is known as the Children's Hour.

I hear in the chamber above me
　　The patter of little feet,
The sound of a door that is opened,
　　And voices soft and sweet.

From my study I see in the lamplight,
　　Descending the broad hall stair,
Grave Alice, and laughing Allegra,
　　And Edith with golden hair.

A whisper, and then a silence:
  Yet I know by their merry eyes
They are plotting and planning together
  To take me by surprise.

A sudden rush from the stairway,
  A sudden raid from the hall!
By three doors left unguarded
  They enter my castle wall!

They climb up into my turret
  O'er the arms and back of my chair;
If I try to escape, they surround me;
  They seem to be everywhere.

They almost devour me with kisses,
  Their arms about me entwine,
Till I think of the Bishop of Bingen
  In his Mouse-Tower on the Rhine!

Do you think, O blue-eyed banditti,
  Because you have scaled the wall,
Such an old moustache as I am
  Is not a match for you all!

I have you fast in my fortress,
  And will not let you depart,
But put you down into the dungeon
  In the round-tower of my heart.

And there will I keep you forever,
  Yes, forever and a day,
Till the walls shall crumble to ruin,
  And moulder in dust away!

From *The Song of Hiawatha*

Introduction

Should you ask me, whence these stories?
  Whence these legends and traditions,
With the odors of the forest,
With the dew and damp of meadows,
With the curling smoke of wigwams,
With the rushing of great rivers,
With their frequent repetitions,
And their wild reverberations,
As of thunder in the mountains?
I should answer, I should tell you,
  "From the forests and the prairies,
From the great lakes of the Northland,
From the land of the Ojibways,
From the land of the Dacotahs,
From the mountains, moors, and fen-lands
Where the heron, the Shuh-shuh-gah,
Feeds among the reeds and rushes.
I repeat them as I heard them
From the lips of Nawadaha,
The musician, the sweet singer."
  Should you ask where Nawadaha
Found these songs so wild and wayward,
Found these legends and traditions,
I should answer, I should tell you,
"In the bird's-nests of the forest,
In the lodges of the beaver,
In the hoof-prints of the bison,
In the eyry of the eagle!
  "All the wild-fowl sang them to him,
In the moorlands and the fen-lands,

In the melancholy marshes;
Chetowaik, the plover, sang them,
Mahng, the loon, the wild-goose, Wawa,
The blue heron, the Shuh-shuh-gah,
And the grouse, the Mushkodasa!"
    If still further you should ask me,
Saying, "Who was Nawadaha?
Tell us of this Nawadaha,"
I should answer your inquiries
Straightway in such words as follow.
    "In the vale of Tawasentha,
In the green and silent valley,
By the pleasant water-courses,
Dwelt the singer Nawadaha.
Round about the Indian village
Spread the meadows and the cornfields,
And beyond them stood the forest,
Stood the groves of singing pinetrees,
Green in Summer, white in Winter,
Ever sighing, ever singing.
    "And the pleasant water-courses,
You could trace them through the valley,
By the rushing in the Spring-time,
By the alders in the Summer,
By the white fog in the Autumn,
By the black line in the Winter;
And beside them dwelt the singer,
In the vale of Tawasentha,
In the green and silent valley.
    "There he sang of Hiawatha,
Sang the Song of Hiawatha,
Sang his wondrous birth and being,
How he prayed and how he fasted,

How he lived, and toiled, and suffered,
That the tribes of men might prosper,
That he might advance his people!"
　Ye who love the haunts of Nature,
Love the sunshine of the meadow,
Love the shadow of the forest,
Love the wind among the branches,
And the rain-shower and the snowstorm,
And the rushing of great rivers
Through their palisades of pinetrees,
And the thunder in the mountains,
Whose innumerable echoes
Flap like eagles in their eyries;—
Listen to these wild traditions,
To this Song of Hiawatha!
　Ye who love a nation's legends,
Love the ballads of a people,
That like voices from afar off
Call to us to pause and listen,
Speak in tones so plain and childlike,
Scarcely can the ear distinguish
Whether they are sung or spoken;—
Listen to this Indian Legend,
To this Song of Hiawatha!
　Ye whose hearts are fresh and simple,
Who have faith in God and Nature,
Who believe that in all ages
Every human heart is human,
That in even savage bosoms
There are longings, yearnings, strivings
For the good they comprehend not,
That the feeble hands and helpless,
Groping blindly in the darkness,

Touch God's right hand in that darkness
And are lifted up and strengthened;—
Listen to this simple story,
To this Song of Hiawatha!
   Ye, who sometimes, in your rambles
Through the green lanes of the country,
Where the tangled barberry-bushes
Hang their tufts of crimson berries
Over stone walls gray with mosses,
Pause by some neglected graveyard,
For a while to muse, and ponder
On a half effaced inscription,
Written with little skill of song-craft,
Homely phrases, but each letter
Full of hope and yet of heart-break,
Full of all the tender pathos
Of the Here and the Hereafter;—
Stay and read this rude inscription,
Read this Song of Hiawatha!

Paul Revere's Ride

Listen, my children, and you shall hear
Of the midnight ride of Paul Revere,
On the eighteenth of April, in Seventy-five;
Hardly a man is now alive
Who remembers that famous day and year.
He said to his friend, "If the British march
By land or sea from the town tonight,
Hang a lantern aloft in the belfry arch
Of the North Church tower as a signal light,—
One, if by land, and two, if by sea;

And I on the opposite shore will be,
Ready to ride and spread the alarm
Through every Middlesex village and farm,
    For the country folk to be up and to arm."

Then he said, "Good night!" and with muffled oar
Silently rowed to the Charlestown shore,
Just as the moon rose over the bay,
Where swinging wide at her moorings lay
The Somerset, British man-of-war;
A phantom ship, with each mast and spar
Across the moon like a prison bar,
And a huge black hulk, that was magnified
By its own reflection in the tide.
Meanwhile, his friend, through alley and street,
Wanders and watches with eager ears,
Till in the silence around him he hears
The muster of men at the barrack door,
The sound of arms, and the tramp of feet,
And the measured tread of the grenadiers,
Marching down to their boats on the shore.

Then he climbed the tower of the Old North Church,
By the wooden stairs, with stealthy tread,
To the belfry-chamber overhead,
And startled the pigeons from their perch
On the sombre rafters, that round him made
Masses and moving shapes of shade,—
By the trembling ladder, steep and tall,
To the highest window in the wall,
Where he paused to listen and look down
A moment on the roofs of the town,
And the moonlight flowing over all.

Beneath, in the churchyard, lay the dead,
In their night-encampment on the hill,
Wrapped in silence so deep and still
That he could hear, like a sentinel's tread,
The watchful night-wind, as it went
Creeping along from tent to tent,
And seeming to whisper, "All is well!"
A moment only he feels the spell
Of the place and the hour, and the secret dread
Of the lonely belfry and the dead;
For suddenly all his thoughts are bent
On a shadowy something far away,
Where the river widens to meet the bay,—
A line of black that bends and floats
On the rising tide, like a bridge of boats.

Meanwhile, impatient to mount and ride,
Booted and spurred, with a heavy stride
On the opposite shore walked Paul Revere.
Now he patted his horse's side,
Now gazed at the landscape far and near,
Then, impetuous, stamped the earth,
And turned and tightened his saddle-girth;
But mostly he watched with eager search
The belfry-tower of the Old North Church,
As it rose above the graves on the hill,
Lonely and spectral and sombre and still.
And lo! as he looks, on the belfry's height
A glimmer, and then a stream of light!
He springs to the saddle, the bridle he turns,
But lingers and gazes, till full on his sight
A second lamp in the belfry burns!

A hurry of hoofs in a village street,
A shape in the moonlight, a bulk in the dark,
And beneath, from the pebbles, in passing, a spark
Struck out by a steed flying fearless and fleet:
That was all! And yet, through the gloom and the light,
The fate of a nation was riding that night;
And the spark struck out by that steed, in his flight,
Kindled the land into flame with its heat.

He has left the village and mounted the steep,
And beneath him, tranquil and broad and deep,
Is the Mystic, meeting the ocean tides;
And under the alders that skirt its edge,
Now soft on the sand, now loud on the ledge,
Is heard the tramp of his steed as he rides.

It was twelve by the village clock,
When he crossed the bridge into Medford town.
He heard the crowing of the cock,
And the barking of the farmer's dog,
And felt the damp of the river fog,
That rises after the sun goes down.

It was one by the village clock,
When he galloped into Lexington.
He saw the gilded weathercock
Swim in the moonlight as he passed,
And the meeting-house windows, blank and bare,
Gaze at him with a spectral glare,
As if they already stood aghast
At the bloody work they would look upon.

It was two by the village clock,
When he came to the bridge in Concord town.
He heard the bleating of the flock,
And the twitter of birds among the trees,
And felt the breath of the morning breeze
Blowing over the meadows brown.
And one was safe and asleep in his bed
Who at the bridge would be first to fall,
Who that day would be lying dead,
Pierced by a British musket-ball.

You know the rest. In the books you have read,
How the British Regulars fired and fled,—
How the farmers gave them ball for ball,
From behind each fence and farmyard wall,
Chasing the red-coats down the lane,
Then crossing the fields to emerge again
Under the trees at the turn of the road,
And only pausing to fire and load.

So through the night rode Paul Revere;
And so through the night went his cry of alarm
To every Middlesex village and farm,—
A cry of defiance and not of fear,
A voice in the darkness, a knock at the door,
And a word that shall echo forevermore!
For, borne on the night-wind of the Past,
Through all our history, to the last,
In the hour of darkness and peril and need,
The people will waken and listen to hear
The hurrying hoof-beats of that steed,
And the midnight message of Paul Revere.

The Wreck of the Hesperus

It was the schooner Hesperus,
    That sailed the wintry sea;
And the skipper had taken his little daughtèr,
    To bear him company.

Blue were her eyes as the fairy-flax,
    Her cheeks like the dawn of day,
And her bosom white as the hawthorn buds,
    That ope in the month of May.

The skipper he stood beside the helm,
    His pipe was in his mouth,
And he watched how the veering flaw did blow
    The smoke now West, now South.

Then up and spake an old Sailòr,
    Had sailed the Spanish Main,
"I pray thee, put into yonder port,
    For I fear a hurricane.

"Last night, the moon had a golden ring,
    And to-night no moon we see!"
The skipper, he blew a whiff from his pipe,
    And a scornful laugh laughed he.

Colder and louder blew the wind,
    A gale from the Northeast;
The snow fell hissing in the brine,
    And the billows frothed like yeast.

Down came the storm, and smote amain,
    The vessel in its strength;
She shuddered and paused, like a frighted steed,
    Then leaped her cable's length.

"Come hither! come hither! my little daughtèr,
     And do not tremble so;
For I can weather the roughest gale,
     That ever wind did blow."

He wrapped her warm in his seaman's coat
     Against the stinging blast;
He cut a rope from a broken spar,
     And bound her to the mast.

"O father! I hear the church-bells ring,
     O say, what may it be?"
"'T is a fog-bell on a rock-bound coast!"—
     And he steered for the open sea.

"O father! I hear the sound of guns,
     O say, what may it be?"
"Some ship in distress, that cannot live
     In such an angry sea!"

"O father! I see a gleaming light,
     O say, what may it be?"
But the father answered never a word,
     A frozen corpse was he.

Lashed to the helm, all stiff and stark,
     With his face turned to the skies,
The lantern gleamed through the gleaming snow
     On his fixed and glassy eyes.

Then the maiden clasped her hands and prayed
     That savèd she might be;
And she thought of Christ, who stilled the wave
     On the Lake of Galilee.

And fast through the midnight dark and drear,
    Through the whistling sleet and snow,
Like a sheeted ghost, the vessel swept
    Towards the reef of Norman's Woe.

And ever the fitful gusts between
    A sound came from the land;
It was the sound of the trampling surf,
    On the rocks and the hard sea-sand.

The breakers were right beneath her bows,
    She drifted a dreary wreck,
And a whooping billow swept the crew
    Like icicles from her deck.

She struck where the white and fleecy waves
    Looked soft as carded wool,
But the cruel rocks, they gored her side
    Like the horns of an angry bull.

Her rattling shrouds, all sheathed in ice,
    With the masts went by the board;
Like a vessel of glass, she stove and sank,
    Ho! ho! the breakers roared!

At daybreak, on the bleak sea-beach,
    A fisherman stood aghast,
To see the form of a maiden fair,
    Lashed close to a drifting mast.

The salt-sea was frozen on her breast,
    The salt tears in her eyes;
And he saw her hair, like the brown sea-weed,
    On the billows fall and rise.

Such was the wreck of the Hesperus,
  In the midnight and the snow!
Christ save us all from a death like this,
  On the reef of Norman's Woe!

The Day is Done

The day is done, and the darkness
  Falls from the wings of Night,
As a feather is wafted downward
  From an eagle in his flight.

I see the lights of the village
  Gleam through the rain and the mist,
And a feeling of sadness comes o'er me
  That my soul cannot resist:

A feeling of sadness and longing,
  That is not akin to pain,
And resembles sorrow only
  As the mist resembles the rain.

Come, read to me some poem,
  Some simple and heartfelt lay,
That shall soothe this restless feeling,
  And banish the thoughts of day.

Not from the grand old masters,
  Not from the bards sublime,
Whose distant footsteps echo
  Through the corridors of Time.

For, like strains of martial music,
  Their mighty thoughts suggest
Life's endless toil and endeavor;
  And to-night I long for rest.

Read from some humbler poet,
    Whose songs gushed from his heart,
As showers from the clouds of summer,
    Or tears from the eyelids start;

Who, through long days of labor,
    And nights devoid of ease,
Still heard in his soul the music
    Of wonderful melodies.

Such songs have power to quiet
    The restless pulse of care,
And come like the benediction
    That follows after prayer.

Then read from the treasured volume
    The poem of thy choice,
And lend to the rhyme of the poet
    The beauty of thy voice.

And the night shall be filled with music,
    And the cares, that infest the day,
Shall fold their tents, like the Arabs,
    And as silently steal away.

Excelsior

The shades of night were falling fast,
As through an Alpine village passed
A youth, who bore, 'mid snow and ice,
A banner with the strange device
        Excelsior!

His brow was sad; his eye beneath,
Flashed like a faulchion from its sheath,
And like a silver clarion rung
The accents of that unknown tongue,
    Excelsior!

In happy homes he saw the light
Of household fires gleam warm and bright;
Above, the spectral glaciers shone,
And from his lips escaped a groan,
    Excelsior!

"Try not the Pass!" the old man said;
"Dark lowers the tempest overhead,
The roaring torrent is deep and wide!"
And loud that clarion voice replied
    Excelsior!

"O stay," the maiden said, "and rest
Thy weary head upon this breast!"
A tear stood in his bright blue eye,
But still he answered, with a sigh,
    Excelsior!

"Beware the pine-tree's withered branch!
Beware the awful avalanche!"
This was the peasant's last Good-night,
A voice replied, far up the height,
    Excelsior!

At break of day, as heavenward
The pious monks of Saint Bernard
Uttered the oft-repeated prayer,
A voice cried through the startled air
    Excelsior!

A traveller, by the faithful hound,
Half-buried in the snow was found,
Still grasping in his hand of ice
That banner with the strange device
    Excelsior!

There in the twilight cold and gray,
Lifeless, but beautiful, he lay,
And from the sky, serene and far,
A voice fell, like a falling star,
    Excelsior!

My Lost Youth

Often I think of the beautiful town
    That is seated by the sea;
Often in thought go up and down
The pleasant streets of that dear old town,
   And my youth comes back to me.
    And a verse of a Lapland song
    Is haunting my memory still:
"A boy's will is the wind's will,
And the thoughts of youth are long, long thoughts."

I can see the shadowy lines of its trees,
   And catch, in sudden gleams,
The sheen of the far-surrounding seas,
And islands that were the Hesperides
   Of all my boyish dreams.
    And the burden of that old song,
    It murmurs and whispers still:
"A boy's will is the wind's will,
And the thoughts of youth are long, long thoughts."

I remember the black wharves and the slips,
　　And the sea-tides tossing free;
And Spanish sailors with bearded lips,
And the beauty and mystery of the ships,
　　And the magic of the sea.
　　　　And the voice of that wayward song
　　　　Is singing and saying still:
　　"A boy's will is the wind's will,
And the thoughts of youth are long, long thoughts."

I remember the bulwarks by the shore,
And the fort upon the hill;
The sun-rise gun, with its hollow roar,
The drum-beat repeated o'er and o'er,
　　And the bugle wild and shrill.
　　　　And the music of that old song
　　　　Throbs in my memory still:
　　"A boy's will is the wind's will,
And the thoughts of youth are long, long thoughts."

I remember the sea-fight far away,
　　How it thundered o'er the tide!
And the dead captains, as they lay
In their graves, o'erlooking the tranquil bay,
　　Where they in battle died.
　　　　And the sound of that mournful song
　　　　Goes through me with a thrill:
　　"A boy's will is the wind's will,
And the thoughts of youth are long, long thoughts."

I can see the breezy dome of groves,
　　The shadows of Deering's Woods;
And the friendships old and the early loves
Come back with a Sabbath sound, as of doves

In quiet neighborhoods.
   And the verse of that sweet old song,
     It flutters and murmurs still:
"A boy's will is the wind's will,
And the thoughts of youth are long, long thoughts."

I remember the gleams and glooms that dart
   Across the schoolboy's brain;
The song and the silence in the heart,
That in part are prophecies, and in part
   Are longings wild and vain.
     And the voice of that fitful song
     Sings on, and is never still:
"A boy's will is the wind's will,
And the thoughts of youth are long, long thoughts."

There are things of which I may not speak;
   There are dreams that cannot die;
There are thoughts that make the strong heart weak,
And bring a pallor into the cheek,
   And a mist before the eye.
     And the words of that fatal song
     Come over me like a chill:
"A boy's will is the wind's will,
And the thoughts of youth are long, long thoughts."

Strange to me now are the forms I meet
   When I visit the dear old town;
But the native air is pure and sweet,
And the trees that o'ershadow each well-known street,
   As they balance up and down,
     Are singing the beautiful song,
     Are sighing and whispering still:
"A boy's will is the wind's will,
And the thoughts of youth are long, long thoughts."

And Deering's Woods are fresh and fair,
    And with joy that is almost pain
My heart goes back to wander there,
And among the dreams of the days that were,
    I find my lost youth again.
        And the strange and beautiful song,
        The groves are repeating it still:
    "A boy's will is the wind's will,
And the thoughts of youth are long, long thoughts."

The Cross of Snow

In the long, sleepless watches of the night,
    A gentle face—the face of one long dead—
    Looks at me from the wall, where round its head
    The night-lamp casts a halo of pale light.
Here in this room she died; and soul more white
    Never through martyrdom of fire was led
    To its repose; nor can in books be read
    The legend of a life more benedight.
There is a mountain in the distant West
    That, sun-defying, in its deep ravines
    Displays a cross of snow upon its side.
Such is the cross I wear upon my breast
    These eighteen years, through all the changing scenes
    And seasons, changeless since the day she died.

Hymn to the Night

I heard the trailing garments of the Night
    Sweep through her marble halls!
I saw her sable skirts all fringed with light
    From the celestial walls!

I felt her presence, by its spell of might,
    Stoop o'er me from above;
The calm, majestic presence of the Night,
    As of the one I love.

I heard the sounds of sorrow and delight,
    The manifold, soft chimes,
That fill the haunted chambers of the Night,
    Like some old poet's rhymes.

From the cool cisterns of the midnight air
    My spirit drank repose;
The fountain of perpetual peace flows there,—
    From those deep cisterns flows.

O holy Night! from thee I learn to bear
    What man has borne before!
Thou layest thy finger on the lips of Care,
    And they complain no more.

Peace! Peace! Orestes-like I breathe this prayer!
    Descend with broad-winged flight,
The welcome, the thrice-prayed for, the most fair,
    The best-beloved Night!

Mezzo Cammin

Boppard on the Rhine. August 25, 1842

Half of my life is gone, and I have let
   The years slip from me and have not fulfilled
   The aspiration of my youth, to build
   Some tower of song with lofty parapet.
Not indolence, nor pleasure, nor the fret
   Of restless passions that would not be stilled,
   But sorrow, and a care that almost killed,
   Kept me from what I may accomplish yet;
Though, half-way up the hill, I see the Past
   Lying beneath me with its sounds and sights,—
   A city in the twilight dim and vast,
With smoking roofs, soft bells, and gleaming lights,—
   And hear above me on the autumnal blast
   The cataract of Death far thundering from the heights.

JOHN GREENLEAF WHITTIER

1807-1892

What the Birds Said

The birds against the April wind
   Flew northward, singing as they flew;
They sang, "The land we leave behind
   Has swords for corn-blades, blood for dew."

"O wild-birds, flying from the South,
   What saw and heard ye, gazing down?"
"We saw the mortar's upturned mouth,
   The sickened camp, the blazing town!

"Beneath the bivouac's starry lamps,
   We saw your march-worn children die;
In shrouds of moss, in cypress swamps,
   We saw your dead uncoffined lie.

"We heard the starving prisoner's sighs,
   And saw, from line and trench, your sons
Follow our flight with home-sick eyes
   Beyond the battery's smoking guns."

"And heard and saw ye only wrong
   And pain," I cried, "O wing-worn flocks?"
"We heard," they sang, "the freedman's song,
   The crash of Slavery's broken locks!

"We saw from new, uprising States
   The treason-nursing mischief spurned,
As, crowding Freedom's ample gates,
   The long-estranged and lost returned.

"O'er dusky faces, seamed and old,
   And hands horn-hard with unpaid toil,
With hope in every rustling fold,
   We saw your star-dropt flag uncoil.

"And struggling up through sounds accursed,
  A grateful murmur clomb the air;
A whisper scarcely heard at first,
  It filled the listening heavens with prayer.

"And sweet and far, as from a star,
  Replied a voice which shall not cease,
Till, drowning all the noise of war,
  It sings the blessed song of peace!"

So to me, in a doubtful day
  Of chill and slowly greening spring,
Low stooping from the cloudy gray,
  The wild-birds sang or seemed to sing.

They vanished in the misty air,
  The song went with them in their flight;
But lo! they left the sunset fair,
  And in the evening there was light.

Barbara Frietchie

Up from the meadows rich with corn,
Clear in the cool September morn,

The clustered spires of Frederick stand
Green-walled by the hills of Maryland.

Round about them orchards sweep,
Apple and peach trees fruited deep,

Fair as the garden of the Lord
To the eyes of the famished rebel horde,

On that pleasant morn of the early fall
When Lee marched over the mountain-wall;

Over the mountains winding down,
Horse and foot, into Frederick town.

Forty flags with their silver stars,
Forty flags with their crimson bars,

Flapped in the morning wind: the sun
Of noon looked down, and saw not one.

Up rose old Barbara Frietchie then,
Bowed with her fourscore years and ten;

Bravest of all in Frederick town,
She took up the flag the men hauled down;

In her attic window the staff she set,
To show that one heart was loyal yet.

Up the street came the rebel tread,
Stonewall Jackson riding ahead.

Under his slouched hat left and right
He glanced; the old flag met his sight.

"Halt!"—the dust-brown ranks stood fast.
"Fire!"—out blazed the rifle-blast.

It shivered the window, pane and sash;
It rent the banner with seam and gash.

Quick, as it fell, from the broken staff
Dame Barbara snatched the silken scarf.

She leaned far out on the window-sill,
And shook it forth with a royal will.

"Shoot, if you must, this old gray head,
But spare your country's flag," she said.

A shade of sadness, a blush of shame,
Over the face of the leader came;

The nobler nature within him stirred
To life at that woman's deed and word;

"Who touches a hair of yon gray head
Dies like a dog! March on!" he said.

All day long through Frederick street
Sounded the tread of marching feet:

All day long that free flag tost
Over the heads of the rebel host.

Ever its torn folds rose and fell
On the loyal winds that loved it well;

And through the hill-gaps sunset light
Shone over it with a warm good-night.

Barbara Frietchie's work is o'er,
And the Rebel rides on his raids no more.

Honor to her! and let a tear
Fall, for her sake, on Stonewall's bier.

Over Barbara Frietchie's grave,
Flag of Freedom and Union, wave!

Peace and order and beauty draw
Round thy symbol of light and law;

And ever the stars above look down
On thy stars below in Frederick town!

Snow-Bound

A Winter Idyl

The sun that brief December day
Rose cheerless over hills of gray,
And, darkly circled, gave at noon
A sadder light than waning moon.
Slow tracing down the thickening sky
Its mute and ominous prophecy,
A portent seeming less than threat,
It sank from sight before it set.
A chill no coat, however stout,
Of homespun stuff could quite shut out,
A hard, dull bitterness of cold,
   That checked, mid-vein, the circling race
   Of life-blood in the sharpened face,
The coming of the snow-storm told.
The wind blew east: we heard the roar
Of Ocean on his wintry shore,
And felt the strong pulse throbbing there
Beat with low rhythm our inland air.

Meanwhile we did our nightly chores,—
Brought in the wood from out of doors,
Littered the stalls, and from the mows
Raked down the herd's-grass for the cows;
Heard the horse whinnying for his corn;
And, sharply clashing horn on horn,
Impatient down the stanchion rows
The cattle shake their walnut bows;
While, peering from his early perch
Upon the scaffold's pole of birch,
The cock his crested helmet bent
And down his querulous challenge sent.

Unwarmed by any sunset light
The gray day darkened into night,
A night made hoary with the swarm
And whirl-dance of the blinding storm,
As zigzag wavering to and fro
Crossed and recrossed the wingéd snow:
And ere the early bed-time came
The white drift piled the window-frame,
And through the glass the clothes-line posts
Looked in like tall and sheeted ghosts.
So all night long the storm roared on:
The morning broke without a sun;
In tiny spherule traced with lines
Of Nature's geometric signs,
In starry flake, and pellicle,
All day the hoary meteor fell;
And, when the second morning shone,
We looked upon a world unknown,
On nothing we could call our own.
Around the glistening wonder bent
The blue walls of the firmament,
No cloud above, no earth below,—
A universe of sky and snow!
The old familiar sights of ours
Took marvellous shapes; strange domes and towers
Rose up where sty or corn-crib stood,
Or garden wall, or belt of wood;
A smooth white mound the brush-pile showed,
A fenceless drift what once was road;
The bridle-post an old man sat
With loose-flung coat and high cocked hat;

The well-curb had a Chinese roof;
And even the long sweep, high aloof,
In its slant splendor, seemed to tell
Of Pisa's leaning miracle.

A prompt, decisive man, no breath
Our father wasted: "Boys, a path!"
Well pleased, (for when did farmer boy
Count such a summons less than joy?)
Our buskins on our feet we drew;
    With mittened hands, and caps drawn low,
    To guard our necks and ears from snow,
We cut the solid whiteness through.
And, where the drift was deepest, made
A tunnel walled and overlaid
With dazzling crystal: we had read
Of rare Aladdin's wondrous cave,
And to our own his name we gave,
With many a wish the luck were ours
To test his lamp's supernal powers.
We reached the barn with merry din,
And roused the prisoned brutes within.
The old horse thrust his long head out,
And grave with wonder gazed about;
The cock his lusty greeting said,
And forth his speckled harem led;
The oxen lashed their tails, and hooked,
And mild reproach of hunger looked;
The hornéd patriarch of the sheep,
Like Egypt's Amun roused from sleep,
Shook his sage head with gesture mute,
And emphasized with stamp of foot.

All day the gusty north-wind bore
The loosening drift its breath before;
Low circling round its southern zone,
The sun through dazzling snow-mist shone.
No church-bell lent its Christian tone
To the savage air, no social smoke
Curled over woods of snow-hung oak.
A solitude made more intense
By dreary voicéd elements,
The shrieking of the mindless wind,
The moaning tree-boughs swaying blind,
And on the glass the unmeaning beat
Of ghostly finger-tips of sleet.
Beyond the circle of our hearth
No welcome sound of toil or mirth
Unbound the spell, and testified
Of human life and thought outside.
We minded that the sharpest ear
The buried brooklet could not hear,
The music of whose liquid lip
Had been to us companionship,
And, in our lonely life, had grown
To have an almost human tone.

As night drew on, and, from the crest
Of wooded knolls that ridged the west,
The sun, a snow-blown traveller, sank
From sight beneath the smothering bank,
We piled, with care, our nightly stack
Of wood against the chimney-back,—
The oaken log, green, huge, and thick,
And on its top the stout back-stick;
The knotty forestick laid apart,

And filled between with curious art
The ragged brush; then, hovering near,
We watched the first red blaze appear,
Heard the sharp crackle, caught the gleam
On whitewashed wall and sagging beam,
Until the old, rude-furnished room
Burst, flower-like, into rosy bloom;
While radiant with a mimic flame
Outside the sparkling drift became,
And through the bare-boughed lilac-tree
Our own warm hearth seemed blazing free.
The crane and pendent trammels showed,
The Turks' heads on the andirons glowed;
While childish fancy, prompt to tell
The meaning of the miracle,
Whispered the old rhyme: "*Under the tree,*
When fire outdoors burns merrily.
There the witches are making tea."

The moon above the eastern wood
Shone at its full; the hill-range stood
Transfigured in the silver flood,
Its blown snows flashing cold and keen,
Dead white, save where some sharp ravine
Took shadow, or the sombre green
Of hemlocks turned to pitchy black
Against the whiteness at their back.
For such a world and such a night
Most fitting that unwarming light,
Which only seemed where'er it fell
To make the coldness visible.

Shut in from all the world without,
We sat the clean-winged hearth about,
Content to let the north-wind roar
In baffled rage at pane and door,
While the red logs before us beat
The frost-line back with tropic heat;
And ever, when a louder blast
Shook beam and rafter as it passed,
The merrier up its roaring draught
The great throat of the chimney laughed.
The house-dog on his paws outspread
Laid to the fire his drowsy head,
The cat's dark silhouette on the wall
A couchant tiger's seemed to fall;
And, for the winter fireside meet,
Between the andirons' straddling feet,
The mug of cider simmered slow,
The apples sputtered in a row,
And, close at hand, the basket stood
With nuts from brown October's wood.

What matter how the night behaved?
What matter how the north-wind raved?
Blow high, blow low, not all its snow
Could quench our hearth-fire's ruddy glow.
O Time and Change!—with hair as gray
As was my sire's that winter day,
How strange it seems, with so much gone
Of life and love, to still live on!
Ah, brother! only I and thou
Are left of all that circle now,—
The dear home faces whereupon
That fitful firelight paled and shone.

Henceforward, listen as we will,
The voices of that hearth are still;
Look where we may, the wide earth o'er,
Those lighted faces smile no more.
We tread the paths their feet have worn,
    We sit beneath their orchard-trees,
    We hear, like them, the hum of bees
And rustle of the bladed corn;
We turn the pages that they read,
    Their written words we linger o'er,
But in the sun they cast no shade,
No voice is heard, no sign is made,
    No step is on the conscious floor!
Yet Love will dream, and Faith will trust,
(Since He who knows our need is just,)
That somehow, somewhere, meet we must.
Alas for him who never sees
The stars shine through his cypress-trees!
Who, hopeless, lays his dead away,
Nor looks to see the breaking day
Across the mournful marbles play!
Who hath not learned, in hours of faith,
    The truth to flesh and sense unknown,
That Life is ever lord of Death,
    And Love can never lose its own!

We sped the time with stories old,
Wrought puzzles out, and riddles told,
Or stammered from our school-book lore
"The Chief of Gambia's golden shore."
How often since, when all the land
Was clay in Slavery's shaping hand,
As if a trumpet called, I've heard

Dame Mercy Warren's rousing word:
"Does not the voice of reason cry,
  Claim the first right which Nature gave,
From the red scourge of bondage fly,
  Nor deign to live a burdened slave!"
Our father rode again his ride
On Memphremagog's wooded side;
Sat down again to moose and samp
In trapper's hut and Indian camp;
Lived o'er the old idyllic ease
Beneath St. François' hemlock-trees;
Again for him the moonlight shone
On Norman cap and bodiced zone;
Again he heard the violin play
Which led the village dance away,
And mingled in its merry whirl
The grandam and the laughing girl.
Or, nearer home, our steps he led
Where Salisbury's level marshes spread
  Mile-wide as flies the laden bee;
Where merry mowers, hale and strong,
Swept, scythe on scythe, their swaths along
  The low green prairies of the sea.
We shared the fishing off Boar's Head,
  And round the rocky Isles of Shoals
  The hake-broil on the drift-wood coals;
The chowder on the sand-beach made,
Dipped by the hungry, steaming hot,
With spoons of clam-shell from the pot.
We heard the tales of witchcraft old,
And dream and sign and marvel told
To sleepy listeners as they lay
Stretched idly on the salted hay,

Adrift along the winding shores,
When favoring breezes designed to blow
The square sail of the gundalow
And idle lay the useless oars.
Our mother, while she turned her wheel
Or run the new-knit stocking-heel,
Told how the Indian hordes came down
At midnight on Cochecho town,
And how her own great-uncle bore
His cruel scalp-mark to fourscore.
Recalling, in her fitting phrase,
   So rich and picturesque and free,
   (The common unrhymed poetry
Of simple life and country ways,)
The story of her early days,—
She made us welcome to her home;
Old hearths grew wide to give us room;
We stole with her a frightened look
At the gray wizard's conjuring-book,
The fame whereof went far and wide
Through all the simple country side;
We heard the hawks at twilight play,
The boat-horn on Piscataqua,
The loon's weird laughter far away;
We fished her little trout-brook, knew
What flowers in wood and meadow grew,
What sunny hillsides autumn-brown
She climbed to shake the ripe nuts down,
Saw where in sheltered cove and bay
The ducks' black squadron anchored lay,
And heard the wild-geese calling loud
Beneath the gray November cloud.

Then, haply, with a look more grave,
And soberer tone, some tale she gave
From painful Sewel's ancient tome,
Beloved in every Quaker home,
Of faith fire-winged by martyrdom,
Or Chalkley's Journal, old and quaint,—
Gentlest of skippers, rare sea-saint!—
Who, when the dreary calms prevailed,
And water-butt and bread-cask failed,
And cruel, hungry eyes pursued
His portly presence mad for food,
With dark hints muttered under breath
Of casting lots for life or death,
Offered, if Heaven withheld supplies,
To be himself the sacrifice.
Then, suddenly, as if to save
The good man from his living grave,
A ripple on the water grew,
A school of porpoise flashed in view.
"Take, eat," he said, "and be content;
These fishes in my stead are sent
By Him who gave the tangled ram
To spare the child of Abraham."

Our uncle, innocent of books,
Was rich in lore of fields and brooks,
The ancient teachers never dumb
Of Nature's unhoused lyceum.
In moons and tides and weather wise,
He read the clouds as prophecies,
And foul or fair could well divine,
By many an occult hint and sign,
Holding the cunning-warded keys
To all the woodcraft mysteries;

Himself to Nature's heart so near
That all her voices in his ear
Of beast or bird had meanings clear,
Like Apollonius of old,
Who knew the tales the sparrows told,
Or Hermes, who interpreted
What the sage cranes of Nilus said;
A simple, guileless, childlike man,
Content to live where life began;
Strong only on his native grounds,
The little world of sights and sounds
Whose girdle was the parish bounds,
Whereof his fondly partial pride
The common features magnified,
As Surrey hills to mountains grew
In White of Selborne's loving view,—
He told how teal and loon he shot,
And how the eagle's eggs he got,
The feats on pond and river done,
The prodigies of rod and gun;
Till, warming with the tales he told,
Forgotten was the outside cold,
The bitter wind unheeded blew,
From ripening corn the pigeons flew,
The partridge drummed i' the wood, the mink
Went fishing down the river-brink.
In fields with bean or clover gay,
The woodchuck, like a hermit gray,
Peered from the doorway of his cell;
The muskrat plied the mason's trade,
And tier by tier his mud-walls laid;
And from the shagbark overhead
The grizzled squirrel dropped his shell.

Next, the dear aunt, whose smile of cheer
And voice in dreams I see and hear,—
The sweetest woman ever Fate
Perverse denied a household mate,
Who, lonely, homeless, not the less
Found peace in love's unselfishness,
And welcome wheresoe'er she went,
A calm and gracious element,
Whose presence seemed the sweet income
And womanly atmosphere of home,—
Called up her girlhood memories,
The huskings and the apple-bees,
The sleigh-rides and the summer sails,
Weaving through all the poor details
And homespun warp of circumstance
A golden woof-thread of romance.
For well she kept her genial mood
And simple faith of maidenhood;
Before her still a cloud-land lay,
The mirage loomed across her way;
The morning dew, that dries so soon
With others, glistened at her noon;
Through years of toil and soil and care
From glossy tress to thin gray hair,
All unprofaned she held apart
The virgin fancies of the heart.
Be shame to him of woman born
Who hath for such but thought of scorn.

There, too, our elder sister plied
Her evening task the stand beside;
A full, rich nature, free to trust,
Truthful and almost sternly just,
Impulsive, earnest, prompt to act,
And make her generous thought a fact,

Keeping with many a light disguise
The secret of self-sacrifice.
O heart sore-tried! thou hast the best
That Heaven itself could give thee,—rest,
Rest from all bitter thoughts and things!
How many a poor one's blessing went
With thee beneath the low green tent
Whose curtain never outward swings!

As one who held herself a part
Of all she saw, and let her heart
Against the household bosom lean,
Upon the motley-braided mat
Our youngest and our dearest sat,
Lifting her large, sweet, asking eyes,
Now bathed within the fadeless green
And holy peace of Paradise.
O, looking from some heavenly hill,
Or from the shade of saintly palms,
Or silver reach of river calms,
Do those large eyes behold me still?
With me one little year ago:—
The chill weight of the winter snow
For months upon her grave has lain;
And now, when summer south-winds blow
And brier and harebell bloom again,
I tread the pleasant paths we trod,
I see the violet-sprinkled sod
Whereon she leaned, too frail and weak
The hillside flowers she loved to seek,
Yet following me where'er I went
With dark eyes full of love's content.
The birds are glad; the brier-rose fills
The air with sweetness; all the hills

Stretch green to June's unclouded sky;
But still I wait with ear and eye
For something gone which should be nigh,
A loss in all familiar things,
In flower that blooms, and bird that sings.
And yet, dear heart! remembering thee,
   Am I not richer than of old?
Safe in thy immortality,
   What change can reach the wealth I hold?
   What chance can mar the pearl and gold
Thy love hath left in trust with me?
And while in life's late afternoon,
   Where cool and long the shadows grow,
I walk to meet the night that soon
   Shall shape and shadow overflow,
I cannot feel that thou art far,
Since near at need the angels are;
And when the sunset gates unbar,
   Shall I not see thee waiting stand,
And, white against the evening star,
   The welcome of thy beckoning hand?

Brisk wielder of the birch and rule,
The master of the district school
Held at the fire his favored place,
Its warm glow lit a laughing face
Fresh-hued and fair, where scarce appeared
The uncertain prophecy of beard.
He teased the mitten-blinded cat,
Played cross-pins on my uncle's hat,
Sang songs, and told us what befalls
In classic Dartmouth's college halls.

Born the wild Northern hills among,
From whence his yeoman father wrung
By patient toil subsistence scant,
Not competence and yet not want,
He early gained the power to pay
His cheerful, self-reliant way;
Could doff at ease his scholar's gown
To peddle wares from town to town;
Or through the long vacation's reach
In lonely lowland districts teach,
Where all the droll experience found
At stranger hearths in boarding round,
The moonlit skater's keen delight,
The sleigh-drive through the frosty night,
The rustic party, with its rough
Accompaniment of blind-man's-buff,
And whirling plate, and forfeits paid,
His winter task a pastime made.
Happy the snow-locked homes wherein
He tuned his merry violin,
Or played the athlete in the barn,
Or held the good dame's winding yarn,
Or mirth-provoking versions told
Of classic legends rare and old,
Wherein the scenes of Greece and Rome
Had all the commonplace of home,
And little seemed at best the odds
'Twixt Yankee pedlers and old gods;
Where Pindus-born Araxes took
The guise of any grist-mill brook,
And dread Olympus at his will
Became a huckleberry hill.

A careless boy that night he seemed;
    But at his desk he had the look
And air of one who wisely schemed,
    And hostage from the future took
    In trainéd thought and lore of book.
Large-brained, clear-eyed,—of such as he
Shall Freedom's young apostles be,
Who, following in War's bloody trail,
Shall every lingering wrong assail;
All chains from limb and spirit strike,
Uplift the black and white alike;
Scatter before their swift advance
The darkness and the ignorance,
The pride, the lust, the squalid sloth,
Which nurtured Treason's monstrous growth,
Made murder pastime, and the hell
Of prison-torture possible;
The cruel lie of caste refute,
Old forms remould, and substitute
For Slavery's lash the freeman's will,
For blind routine, wise-handed skill;
A school-house plant on every hill,
Stretching in radiate nerve-lines thence
The quick wires of intelligence;
Till North and South together brought
Shall own the same electric thought,
In peace a common flag salute,
And, side by side in labor's free
And unresentful rivalry,
Harvest the fields wherein they fought.

Another guest that winter night
Flashed back from lustrous eyes the light.
Unmarked by time, and yet not young,
The honeyed music of her tongue
And words of meekness scarcely told
A nature passionate and bold,
Strong, self-concentred, spurning guide,
Its milder features dwarfed beside
Her unbent will's majestic pride.
She sat among us, at the best,
A not unfeared, half-welcome guest,
Rebuking with her cultured phrase
Our homeliness of words and ways.
A certain pard-like, treacherous grace
  Swayed the lithe limbs and drooped the lash,
  Lent the white teeth their dazzling flash;
  And under low brows, black with night,
  Rayed out at times a dangerous light;
The sharp heat-lightnings of her face
Presaging ill to him whom Fate
Condemned to share her love or hate.
A woman tropical, intense
In thought and act, in soul and sense,
She blended in a like degree
The vixen and the devotee,
Revealing with each freak or feint
  The temper of Petruchio's Kate,
The raptures of Siena's saint.
Her tapering hand and rounded wrist
Had facile power to form a fist;
The warm, dark languish of her eyes
Was never safe from wrath's surprise.

Brows saintly calm and lips devout
Knew every change of scowl and pout;
And the sweet voice had notes more high
And shrill for social battle-cry.

Since then what old cathedral town
Has missed her pilgrim staff and gown,
What convent-gate has held its lock
Against the challenge of her knock!
Through Smyrna's plague-hushed thoroughfares,
Up sea-set Malta's rocky stairs,
Gray olive slopes of hills that hem
Thy tombs and shrines, Jerusalem,
Or startling on her desert throne
The crazy Queen of Lebanon
With claims fantastic as her own,
Her tireless feet have held their way;
And still, unrestful, bowed, and gray,
She watches under Eastern skies,
    With hope each day renewed and fresh,
    The Lord's quick coming in the flesh,
Whereof she dreams and prophesies!

Where'er her troubled path may be,
    The Lord's sweet pity with her go!
The outward wayward life we see,
    The hidden springs we may not know.
Nor is it given us to discern
    What threads the fatal sisters spun,
    Through what ancestral years has run
The sorrow with the woman born,
What forged her cruel chain of moods,
What set her feet in solitudes,
    And held the love within her mute,

What mingled madness in the blood,
  A life-long discord and annoy,
  Water of tears with oil of joy,
And hid within the folded bud
  Perversities of flower and fruit.
It is not ours to separate
The tangled skein of will and fate,
To show what metes and bounds should stand
Upon the soul's debatable land,
And between choice and Providence
Divide the circle of events;
But He who knows our frame is just,
  Merciful, and compassionate,
And full of sweet assurances
And hope for all the language is,
That He remembereth we are dust!

At last the great logs, crumbling low,
Sent out a dull and duller glow,
The bull's-eye watch that hung in view,
Ticking its weary circuit through,
Pointed with mutely-warning sign
Its black hand to the hour of nine.
That sign the pleasant circle broke:
My uncle ceased his pipe to smoke,
Knocked from its bowl the refuse gray
And laid it tenderly away,
Then roused himself to safely cover
The dull red brands with ashes over.
And while, with care, our mother laid
The work aside, her steps she stayed
One moment, seeking to express
Her grateful sense of happiness

For food and shelter, warmth and health,
And love's contentment more than wealth,
With simple wishes (not the weak,
Vain prayers which no fulfilment seek,
But such as warm the generous heart,
O'er-prompt to do with Heaven its part)
That none might lack, that bitter night,
For bread and clothing, warmth and light.

Within our beds awhile we heard
The wind that round the gables roared,
With now and then a ruder shock,
Which made our very bedsteads rock.
We heard the loosened clapboards tost,
The board-nails snapping in the frost;
And on us, through the unplastered wall,
Felt the light sifted snow-flakes fall.
But sleep stole on, as sleep will do
When hearts are light and life is new;
Faint and more faint the murmurs grew,
Till in the summer-land of dreams
They softened to the sound of streams,
Low stir of leaves, and dip of oars,
And lapsing waves on quiet shores.

Next morn we wakened with the shout
Of merry voices high and clear;
And saw the teamsters drawing near
To break the drifted highways out.
Down the long hillside treading slow
We saw the half-buried oxen go,
Shaking the snow from heads uptost,
Their straining nostrils white with frost.
Before our door the straggling train

Drew up, an added team to gain.
The elders threshed their hands a-cold,
    Passed, with the cider-mug, their jokes
    From lip to lip; the younger folks
Down the loose snow-banks, wrestling, rolled,
Then toiled again the cavalcade
    O'er windy hill, through clogged ravine,
    And woodland paths that wound between
Low drooping pine-boughs winter-weighed.
From every barn a team afoot,
At every house a new recruit,
Where, drawn by Nature's subtlest law,
Haply the watchful young men saw
Sweet doorway pictures of the curls
And curious eyes of merry girls,
Lifting their hands in mock defence
Against the snow-ball's compliments,
And reading in each missive tost
The charm with Eden never lost.

We heard once more the sleigh-bells' sound;
    And, following where the teamsters led,
The wise old Doctor went his round,
Just pausing at our door to say,
In the brief autocratic way
Of one who, prompt at Duty's call,
Was free to urge her claim on all,
    That some poor neighbor sick abed
At night our mother's aid would need.
For, one in generous thought and deed,
    What mattered in the sufferer's sight
    The Quaker matron's inward light,
The Doctor's mail of Calvin's creed?

All hearts confess the saints elect
    Who, twain in faith, in love agree,
And melt not in an acid sect
    The Christian pearl of charity!

So days went on: a week had passed
Since the great world was heard from last.
The Almanac we studied o'er,
Read and reread our little store,
Of books and pamphlets, scarce a score;
One harmless novel, mostly hid
From younger eyes, a book forbid,
And poetry, (or good or bad,
A single book was all we had,)
Where Ellwood's meek, drab-skirted Muse,
    A stranger to the heathen Nine,
    Sang, with a somewhat nasal whine,
The wars of David and the Jews.
At last the floundering carrier bore
The village paper to our door.
Lo! broadening outward as we read,
To warmer zones the horizon spread;
In panoramic length unrolled
We saw the marvels that it told.
Before us passed the painted Creeks,
    And daft McGregor on his raids
    In Costa Rica's everglades.
And up Taygetos winding slow
Rode Ypsilanti's Mainote Greeks,
A Turk's head at each saddle-bow!
Welcome to us its week-old news,
Its corner for the rustic Muse,
    Its monthly gauge of snow and rain,

Its record, mingling in a breath
The wedding bell and dirge of death;
Jest, anecdote, and love-lorn tale,
The latest culprit sent to jail;
Its hue and cry of stolen and lost,
Its vendue sales and goods at cost,
  And traffic calling loud for gain.
We felt the stir of hall and street,
The pulse of life that round us beat;
The chill embargo of the snow
Was melted in the genial glow;
Wide swung again our ice-locked door,
And all the world was ours once more!

Clasp, Angel of the backward look
  And folded wings of ashen gray
  And voice of echoes far away,
The brazen covers of thy book;
The weird palimpsest old and vast,
Wherein thou hid'st the spectral past;
Where, closely mingling, pale and glow
The characters of joy and woe;
The monographs of outlived years,
Or smile-illumed or dim with tears,
  Green hills of life that slope to death,
And haunts of home, whose vistaed trees
Shade off to mournful cypresses
  With the white amaranths underneath.
Even while I look, I can but heed
  The restless sands' incessant fall,
Importunate hours that hours succeed,
Each clamorous with its own sharp need,
  And duty keeping pace with all.

Shut down and clasp the heavy lids;
I hear again the voice that bids
The dreamer leave his dream midway
For larger hopes and graver fears:
Life greatens in these later years,
The century's aloe flowers to-day!

Yet, haply, in some lull of life,
Some Truce of God which breaks its strife,
The worldling's eyes shall gather dew,
   Dreaming in throngful city ways
Of winter joys his boyhood knew;
And dear and early friends—the few
Who yet remain—shall pause to view
   These Flemish pictures of old days;
Sit with me by the homestead hearth,
And stretch the hands of memory forth
   To warm them at the wood-fire's blaze!
And thanks untraced to lips unknown
Shall greet me like the odors blown
From unseen meadows newly mown,
Or lilies floating in some pond,
Wood-fringed, the wayside gaze beyond;
The traveller owns the grateful sense
Of sweetness near, he knows not whence,
And, pausing, takes with forehead bare
The benediction of the air.

The Pressed Gentian

The time of gifts has come again,
And, on my northern window-pane,
Outlined against the day's brief light,
A Christmas token hangs in sight.
The wayside travellers, as they pass,
Mark the gray disk of clouded glass;
And the dull blankness seems, perchance,
Folly to their wise ignorance.

They cannot from their outlook see
The perfect grace it hath for me;
For there the flower, whose fringes through
The frosty breath of autumn blew,
Turns from without its face of bloom
To the warm tropic of my room,
And fair as when beside its brook
The hue of bending skies it took.

So from the trodden ways of earth,
Seem some sweet souls who veil their worth,
And offer to the careless glance
The clouding gray of circumstance.
They blossom best where hearth-fires burn,
To loving eyes alone they turn
The flowers of inward grace, that hide
Their beauty from the world outside.

But deeper meanings come to me,
My half-immortal flower, from thee!
Man judges from a partial view,
None ever yet his brother knew;

The Eternal Eye that sees the whole
May better read the darkened soul,
And find, to outward sense denied,
The flower upon its inmost side!

The Trailing Arbutus

I wandered lonely where the pine-trees made
Against the bitter East their barricade,
    And, guided by its sweet
Perfume, I found, within a narrow dell,
The trailing spring flower tinted like a shell
    Amid dry leaves and mosses at my feet.

From under dead boughs, for whose loss the pines
Moaned ceaseless overhead, the blossoming vines
    Lifted their glad surprise,
While yet the bluebird smoothed in leafless trees
His feathers ruffled by the chill sea-breeze,
    And snow-drifts lingered under April skies.

As, pausing, o'er the lonely flower I bent,
I thought of lives thus lowly, clogged and pent,
    Which yet find room,
Through care and cumber, coldness and decay,
To lend a sweetness to the ungenial day,
    And make the sad earth happier for their bloom.

Oliver Wendell Holmes
1809-1894

The Chambered Nautilus

This is the ship of pearl, which, poets feign,
   Sails the unshadowed main,—
   The venturous bark that flings
On the sweet summer wind its purpled wings
In gulfs enchanted, where the Siren sings,
   And coral reefs lie bare,
Where the cold sea-maids rise to sun their streaming hair.

Its webs of living gauze no more unfurl;
   Wrecked is the ship of pearl!
   And every chambered cell,
Where its dim dreaming life was wont to dwell,
As the frail tenant shaped his growing shell,
   Before thee lies revealed,—
Its irised ceiling rent, its sunless crypt unsealed!

Year after year beheld the silent toil
   That spread his lustrous coil;
   Still, as the spiral grew,
He left the past year's dwelling for the new,
Stole with soft step its shining archway through,
   Built up its idle door,
Stretched in his last-found home, and knew the old no more.

Thanks for the heavenly message brought by thee,
   Child of the wandering sea,
   Cast from her lap, forlorn!
From thy dead lips a clearer note is born
Than ever Triton blew from wreathèd horn!
   While on mine ear it rings,
Through the deep caves of thought I hear a voice that sings:—

Build thee more stately mansions, O my soul,
  As the swift seasons roll!
  Leave thy low-vaulted past!
Let each new temple, nobler than the last,
Shut thee from heaven with a dome more vast,
  Till thou at length art free,
Leaving thine outgrown shell by life's unresting sea!

Old Ironsides

Ay, tear her tattered ensign down!
  Long has it waved on high,
And many an eye has danced to see
  That banner in the sky;
Beneath it rung the battle shout,
  And burst the cannon's roar;—
The meteor of the ocean air
  Shall sweep the clouds no more.

Her deck, once red with heroes' blood,
  Where knelt the vanquished foe,
When winds were hurrying o'er the flood,
  And waves were white below,
No more shall feel the victor's tread,
  Or know the conquered knee;—
The harpies of the shore shall pluck
  The eagle of the sea!

Oh, better that her shattered hulk
   Should sink beneath the wave;
Her thunders shook the mighty deep,
   And there should be her grave;
Nail to the mast her holy flag,
   Set every threadbare sail,
And give her to the god of storms,
   The lightning and the gale!

144

ABRAHAM LINCOLN
1809-1865

My Childhood-Home I See Again

My childhood-home I see again,
  And gladden with the view;
And still as mem'ries crowd my brain,
  There's sadness in it too.

O memory! thou mid-way world
  'Twixt Earth and Paradise,
Where things decayed, and loved ones lost
  In dreamy shadows rise.

And freed from all that's gross or vile,
  Seem hallowed, pure, and bright,
Like scenes in some enchanted isle,
  All bathed in liquid light.

As distant mountains please the eye,
  When twilight chases day—
As bugle-tones, that, passing by,
  In distance die away—

As leaving some grand water-fall
  We ling'ring, list it's roar,
So memory will hallow all
  We've known, but know no more.

Now twenty years have passed away,
  Since here I bid farewell
To woods, and fields, and scenes of play
  And school-mates loved so well.

Where many were, how few remain
  Of old familiar things!
But seeing these to mind again
  The lost and absent brings.

The friends I left that parting day—
  How changed, as time has sped!
Young childhood grown, strong manhood grey,
  And half of all are dead.

I hear the lone survivors tell
  How nought from death could save,
Till every sound appears a knell,
  And every spot a grave.

I range the fields with pensive tread,
  And pace the hollow rooms;
And feel (companions of the dead)
  I'm living in the tombs.

And here's an object more of dread,
  Than ought the grave contains—
A human-form, with reason fled,
  While wretched life remains.

Poor Matthew! Once of genius bright,—
  A fortune-favored child—
Now locked for aye, in mental night,
  A haggard mad-man wild.

Poor Matthew! I have ne'er forgot
  When first with maddened will,
Yourself you maimed, your father fought,
  And mother strove to kill;

And terror spread, and neighbours ran,
   Your dang'rous strength to bind;
And soon a howling crazy man,
   Your limbs were fast confined.

How then you writhed and shrieked aloud,
   Your bones and sinnews bared;
And fiendish on the gaping crowd,
   With burning eye-balls glared.

And begged, and swore, and wept, and prayed,
   With maniac laughter joined—
How fearful are the signs displayed,
   By pangs that kill the mind!

And when at length, tho' drear and long,
   Time soothed your fiercer woes—
How plaintively your mournful song,
   Upon the still night rose.

I've heard it oft, as if I dreamed,
   Far-distant, sweet, and lone;
The funeral dirge it ever seemed
   Of reason dead and gone.

To drink it's strains, I've stole away,
   All silently and still,
Ere yet the rising god of day
   Had streaked the Eastern hill.

Air held his breath; the trees all still
   Seemed sorr'wing angels round.
Their swelling tears in dew-drops fell
   Upon the list'ning ground.

But this is past, and nought remains
    That raised you o'er the brute.
Your mad'ning shrieks and soothing strains
    Are like forever mute.

Now fare thee well: more thou the cause
    Than subject now of woe.
All mental pangs, but time's kind laws,
    Hast lost the power to know.

And now away to seek some scene
    Less painful than the last—
With less of horror mingled in
    The present and the past.

The very spot where grew the bread
    That formed my bones, I see.
How strange, old field, on thee to tread,
    And feel I'm part of thee!

EDGAR ALLAN POE
1809-1849

Song

I saw thee on thy bridal day—
    When a burning blush came o'er thee,
Though happiness around thee lay,
    The world all love before thee:

And in thine eye a kindling light
    (Whatever it might be)
Was all on Earth my aching sight
    Of Loveliness could see.

That blush, perhaps, was maiden shame—
    As such it, well may pass—
Though its glow hath raised a fiercer flame
    In the breast of him, alas!

Who saw thee on that bridal day,
    When that deep blush *would* come o'er thee,
Though happiness around thee lay,
    The world all love before thee.

Dreams

Oh! that my young life were a lasting dream!
My spirit not awak'ning till the beam
Of an Eternity should bring the morrow:
Yes! tho' that long dream were of hopeless sorrow,
'Twere better than the dull reality
Of waking life to him whose heart shall be,
And hath been ever, on the chilly earth,
A chaos of deep passion from his birth!

But should it be—that dream eternally
Continuing—as dreams have been to me
In my young boyhood—should it thus be given,
'Twere folly still to hope for higher Heaven!
For I have revell'd, when the sun was bright
In the summer sky; in dreamy fields of light,
And left unheedingly my very heart
In climes of mine imagining—apart
From mine own home, with beings that have been
Of mine own thought—what more could I have seen?

'Twas once and *only* once and the wild hour
From my remembrance shall not pass—some power
Or spell had bound me—'twas the chilly wind
Came o'er me in the night and left behind
Its image on my spirit, or the moon
Shone on my slumbers in her lofty noon
Too coldly—or the stars—howe'er it was
That dream was as that night wind—let it pass.

I have been happy—tho' but in a dream.
I have been happy—and I love the theme—
Dreams! in their vivid colouring of life—
As in that fleeting, shadowy, misty strife
Of semblance with reality which brings
To the delirious eye more lovely things
Of Paradise and Love—and all our own!
Than young Hope in his sunniest hour hath known.

Annabel Lee

It was many and many a year ago,
    In a kingdom by the sea,
That a maiden there lived whom you may know
    By the name of Annabel Lee;—
And this maiden she lived with no other thought
    Than to love and be loved by me.

She was a child and *I* was a child,
    In this kingdom by the sea,
But we loved with a love that was more than love—
    I and my Annabel Lee—
With a love that the wingéd seraphs of Heaven
    Coveted her and me.

And this was the reason that, long ago,
    In this kingdom by the sea,
A wind blew out of a cloud by night
    Chilling my Annabel Lee;
So that her highborn kinsmen came
    And bore her away from me,
To shut her up in a sepulchre
    In this kingdom by the sea.

The angels, not half so happy in Heaven,
    Went envying her and me:—
Yes! that was the reason (as all men know,
    In this kingdom by the sea)
That the wind came out of the cloud, chilling
    And killing my Annabel Lee.

But our love it was stronger by far than the love
    Of those who were older than we—
    Of many far wiser than we—

And neither the angels in Heaven above
   Nor the demons down under the sea
Can ever dissever my soul from the soul
   Of the beautiful Annabel Lee:—

For the moon never beams without bringing me dreams
   Of the beautiful Annabel Lee;
And the stars never rise but I see the bright eyes
   Of the beautiful Annabel Lee;
And so, all the night-tide, I lie down by the side
Of my darling, my darling, my life and my bride
   In her sepulchre there by the sea—
   In her tomb by the side of the sea.

To Helen

Helen, thy beauty is to me
   Like those Nicéan barks of yore,
That gently, o'er a perfumed sea,
   The weary, way-worn wanderer bore
   To his own native shore.

On desperate seas long wont to roam,
   Thy hyacinth hair, thy classic face,
Thy Naiad airs have brought me home
   To the glory that was Greece,
And the grandeur that was Rome.

Lo! in yon brilliant window-niche
   How statue-like I see thee stand,
   The agate lamp within thy hand!
Ah, Psyche, from the regions which
   Are Holy-Land!

A Dream Within a Dream

Take this kiss upon the brow!
And, in parting from you now,
Thus much let me avow:
You are not wrong, who deem
That my days have been a dream;
Yet if hope has flown away
In a night, or in a day,
In a vision, or in none,
Is it therefore the less *gone?*
All that we see or seem
Is but a dream within a dream.

I stand amid the roar
Of a surf-tormented shore,
And I hold within my hand
Grains of the golden sand—
How few! yet how they creep
Through my fingers to the deep,
While I weep—while I weep!
O God! can I not grasp
Them with a tighter clasp?
O God! can I not save
One from the pitiless wave?
Is *all* that we see or seem
But a dream within a dream?

The Raven

Once upon a midnight dreary, while I pondered, weak and weary,
Over many a quaint and curious volume of forgotten lore,
While I nodded, nearly napping, suddenly there came a tapping,
As of some one gently rapping, rapping at my chamber door.
" 'Tis some visiter," I muttered, "tapping at my chamber door—
      Only this, and nothing more."

Ah, distinctly I remember it was in the bleak December,
And each separate dying ember wrought its ghost upon the floor.
Eagerly I wished the morrow;—vainly I had tried to borrow
From my books surcease of sorrow—sorrow for the lost Lenore—
For the rare and radiant maiden whom the angels name Lenore—
      Nameless here for evermore.

And the silken sad uncertain rustling of each purple curtain
Thrilled me—filled me with fantastic terrors never felt before;
So that now, to still the beating of my heart, I stood repeating
" 'Tis some visiter entreating entrance at my chamber door—
Some late visiter entreating entrance at my chamber door;—
      This it is and nothing more."

Presently my soul grew stronger; hesitating then no longer,
"Sir," said I, "or Madam, truly your forgiveness I implore;
But the fact is I was napping, and so gently you came rapping,
And so faintly you came tapping, tapping at my chamber door,
That I scarce was sure I heard you"—here I opened wide the door;—
      Darkness there, and nothing more.

Deep into that darkness peering, long I stood there wondering, fearing,
Doubting, dreaming dreams no mortal ever dared to dream before;
But the silence was unbroken, and the darkness gave no token,
And the only word there spoken was the whispered word, "Lenore!"
This I whispered, and an echo murmured back the word, "Lenore!"
      Merely this, and nothing more.

Then into the chamber turning, all my soul within me burning,
Soon I heard again a tapping somewhat louder than before.
"Surely," said I, "surely that is something at my window lattice;
Let me see, then, what thereat is, and this mystery explore—
Let my heart be still a moment and this mystery explore;—
                'Tis the wind, and nothing more!"

Open here I flung the shutter, when, with many a flirt and flutter,
In there stepped a stately raven of the saintly days of yore;
Not the least obeisance made he; not an instant stopped or stayed he;
But, with mien of lord or lady, perched above my chamber door—
Perched upon a bust of Pallas just above my chamber door—
                Perched, and sat, and nothing more.

Then this ebony bird beguiling my sad fancy into smiling,
By the grave and stem decorum of the countenance it wore,
"Though thy crest be shorn and shaven, thou," I said, "art sure no
    craven,
Ghastly grim and ancient raven wandering from the Nightly shore—
Tell me what thy lordly name is on the Night's Plutonian shore!"
                Quoth the raven, "Nevermore."

Much I marvelled this ungainly fowl to hear discourse so plainly,
Though its answer little meaning—little relevancy bore;
For we cannot help agreeing that no sublunary being
Ever yet was blessed with seeing bird above his chamber door—
Bird or beast upon the sculptured bust above his chamber door,
                With such name as "Nevermore."

But the raven, sitting lonely on the placid bust, spoke only
That one word, as if his soul in that one word he did outpour.
Nothing farther then he uttered—not a feather then he fluttered—
Till I scarcely more than muttered, "Other friends have flown before—
On the morrow he will leave me, as my hopes have flown before."
                Quoth the raven, "Nevermore."

Wondering at the stillness broken by reply so aptly spoken,
"Doubtless," said I, "what it utters is its only stock and store,
Caught from some unhappy master whom unmerciful Disaster
Followed fast and followed faster—so, when Hope he would adjure,
Stern Despair returned, instead of the sweet Hope he dared adjure—
That sad answer, "Nevermore!"

But the raven still beguiling all my sad soul into smiling,
Straight I wheeled a cushioned seat in front of bird, and bust, and door;
Then upon the velvet sinking, I betook myself to linking
Fancy unto fancy, thinking what this ominous bird of yore—
What this grim, ungainly, ghastly, gaunt, and ominous bird of yore
Meant in croaking "Nevermore."

This I sat engaged in guessing, but no syllable expressing
To the fowl whose fiery eyes now burned into my bosom's core;
This and more I sat divining, with my head at ease reclining
On the cushion's velvet lining that the lamplight gloated o'er,
But whose velvet violet lining with the lamplight gloating o'er,
She shall press, ah, nevermore!

Then, methought, the air grew denser, perfumed from an unseen censer
Swung by angels whose faint foot-falls tinkled on the tufted floor.
"Wretch," I cried, "thy God hath lent thee—by these angels he hath
sent thee
Respite—respite and Nepenthe from thy memories of Lenore!
Let me quaff this kind Nepenthe and forget this lost Lenore!"
Quoth the raven, "Nevermore."

"Prophet!" said I, "thing of evil!—prophet still, if bird or devil!—
Whether Tempter sent, or whether tempest tossed thee here ashore,
Desolate, yet all undaunted, on this desert land enchanted—
On this home by Horror haunted—tell me truly, I implore—
Is there—*is* there balm in Gilead?—tell me—tell me, I implore!"
Quoth the raven, "Nevermore."

"Prophet!" said I, "thing of evil!—prophet still, if bird or devil!
By that Heaven that bends above us—by that God we both adore—
Tell this soul with sorrow laden if, within the distant Aidenn,
It shall clasp a sainted maiden whom the angels name Lenore—
Clasp a rare and radiant maiden whom the angels name Lenore."
                    Quoth the raven, "Nevermore."

"Be that word our sign of parting, bird or fiend!" I shrieked, upstarting—
"Get thee back into the tempest and the Night's Plutonian shore!
Leave no black plume as a token of that lie thy soul hath spoken!
Leave my loneliness unbroken!—quit the bust above my door!
Take thy beak from out my heart, and take thy form from off my door!"
                    Quoth the raven, "Nevermore."

And the raven, never flitting, still is sitting, still is sitting
On the pallid bust of Pallas just above my chamber door;
And his eyes have all the seeming of a demon that is dreaming,
And the lamp-light o'er him streaming throws his shadow on the floor;
And my soul from out that shadow that lies floating on the floor
                    Shall be lifted—nevermore!

Ulalume

The skies they were ashen and sober;
    The leaves they were crispèd and sere,
    The leaves they were withering and sere;
It was night in the lonesome October
    Of my most immemorial year;
It was hard by the dim lake of Auber,
    In the misty mid region of Weir:
It was down by the dank tarn of Auber,
    In the ghoul-haunted woodland of Weir.

Here once, through an alley Titanic
 Of cypress, I roamed with my Soul—
 Of cypress, with Psyche, my Soul.
These were days when my heart was volcanic
 As the scoriac rivers that roll,
 As the lavas that restlessly roll
Their sulphurous currents down Yaanek
 In the ultimate climes of the pole,
That groan as they roll down Mount Yaanek
 In the realms of the boreal pole.

Our talk had been serious and sober,
 But our thoughts they were palsied and sere,
 Our memories were treacherous and sere,
For we knew not the month was October,
 And we marked not the night of the year,
 (Ah, night of all nights in the year!)
We noted not the dim lake of Auber
 (Though once we had journeyed down here),
Remembered not the dank tarn of Auber
 Nor the ghoul-haunted woodland of Weir.

And now, as the night was senescent
 And star-dials pointed to morn,
 As the star-dials hinted of morn,
At the end of our path a liquescent
 And nebulous lustre was born,
Out of which a miraculous crescent
 Arose with a duplicate horn,
Astarte's bediamonded crescent
 Distinct with its duplicate horn.

And I said—"She is warmer than Dian:
　　She rolls through an ether of sighs,
　　She revels in a region of sighs:
She has seen that the tears are not dry on
　　These cheeks, where the worm never dies,
And has come past the stars of the Lion
　　To point us the path to the skies,
　　To the Lethean peace of the skies:
Come up, in despite of the Lion,
　　To shine on us with her bright eyes:
Come up through the lair of the Lion,
　　With love in her luminous eyes."

But Psyche, uplifting her finger,
　　Said—"Sadly this star I mistrust,
　　Her pallor I strangely mistrust:
Oh, hasten!—oh, let us not linger!
　　Oh, fly!—let us fly!—for we must."
In terror she spoke, letting sink her
　　Wings until they trailed in the dust;
In agony sobbed, letting sink her
　　Plumes till they trailed in the dust,
　　Till they sorrowfully trailed in the dust.

I replied—"This is nothing but dreaming:
　　Let us on by this tremulous light!
　　Let us bathe in this crystalline light!
Its sibyllic splendor is beaming
　　With hope and in beauty to-night:
　　See, it flickers up the sky through the night!
Ah, we safely may trust to its gleaming,
　　And be sure it will lead us aright:
We safely may trust to a gleaming
　　That cannot but guide us aright,
　　Since it flickers up to Heaven through the night."

Thus I pacified Psyche and kissed her,
　　And tempted her out of her gloom,
　　And conquered her scruples and gloom;
And we passed to the end of the vista,
　　But were stopped by the door of a tomb,
　　By the door of a legended tomb;
And I said—"What is written, sweet sister,
　　On the door of this legended tomb?"
　　She replied—"Ulalume—Ulalume—
　　'Tis the vault of thy lost Ulalume!"

Then my heart it grew ashen and sober
　　As the leaves that were crispèd and sere,
　　As the leaves that were withering and sere,
And I cried—"It was surely October
　　On this very night of last year
　　That I journey—I journey down here,
　　That I brought a dread burden down here:
　　On this night of all nights in the year,
　　Ah, what demon has tempted me here?
Well I know, now, this dim lake of Auber,
　　This misty mid region of Weir:
Well I know, now, this dank tarn of Auber,
　　This ghoul-haunted woodland of Weir."

Sonnet—Silence

There are some qualities—some incorporate things,
　　That have a double life, which thus is made
A type of that twin entity which springs
　　From matter and light, evinced in solid and shade.
There is a two-fold *Silence*—sea and shore—
　　Body and Soul. One dwells in lonely places,
　　Newly with grass o'ergrown; some solemn graces,

Some human memories and tearful lore,
Render him terrorless: his name's "No more."
He is the corporate Silence: dread him not!
    No power hath he of evil in himself;
But should some urgent fate (untimely lot!)
    Bring thee to meet his shadow (nameless elf,
That haunteth the lone regions where hath trod
No foot of man,) commend thyself to God!

Sonnet—To Science

Science! true daughter of old Time thou art!
    Who alterest all things with thy peering eyes.
Why preyest thou thus upon the poet's heart,
    Vulture, whose wings are dull realities?
How should he love thee? or how deem thee wise,
    Who wouldst not leave him in his wandering
To seek for treasure in the jeweled skies,
    Albeit he soared with an undaunted wing?
Hast thou not dragged Diana from her car,
    And driven the hamadryad from the wood
To seek a shelter in some happier star?
    Hast thou not torn the naiad from her flood,
The elfin from the green grass, and from me
The summer dream beneath the tamarind tree?

The Haunted Palace

In the greenest of our valleys
   By good angels tenanted,
Once a fair and stately palace—
   Radiant palace—reared its head.
In the monarch Thought's dominion,
   It stood there!
Never seraph spread a pinion
   Over fabric half so fair!

Banners yellow, glorious, golden,
   On its roof did float and flow
(This—all this—was in the olden
   Time long ago),
And every gentle air that dallied,
   In that sweet day,
Along the ramparts plumed and pallid,
   A wingèd odor went away.

Wanderers in that happy valley,
   Through two luminous windows, saw
Spirits moving musically,
   To a lute's well-tunèd law,
Round about a throne where, sitting,
   Porphyrogene!
In state his glory well befitting,
   The ruler of the realm was seen.

And all with pearl and ruby glowing
   Was the fair palace door.
Through which came flowing, flowing, flowing,
   And sparkling evermore,

A troop of Echoes, whose sweet duty
   Was but to sing,
In voices of surpassing beauty,
   The wit and wisdom of their king.

But evil things, in robes of sorrow,
   Assailed the monarch's high estate.
(Ah, let us mourn!—for never morrow
   Shall dawn upon him, desolate!)
And round about his home the glory
   That blushed and bloomed,
Is but a dim-remembered story
   Of the old time entombed.

And travelers, now, within that valley,
   Through the red-litten windows see
Vast forms that move fantastically
   To a discordant melody,
While, like a ghastly rapid river,
   Through the pale door
A hideous throng rush out forever,
   And laugh—but smile no more.

"Stanzas"

How often we forget all time, when lone
Admiring Nature's universal throne;
Her woods—her wilds—her mountains—the intense
Reply of HERS *to* OUR *intelligence!*

1

In youth have I known one with whom the Earth
In secret communing held—as he with it,
In day light, and in beauty from his birth:
Whose fervid, flick'ring torch of life was lit

From the sun and stars, whence he had drawn forth
A passionate light—such for his spirit was fit—
And yet that spirit knew—not in the hour
Of its own fervor—what had o'er it power.

2

Perhaps it may be that my mind is wrought
To a ferver by the moon beam that hangs o'er,
But I will half believe that wild light fraught
With more of sov'reignty than ancient lore
Hath ever told—or is it of a thought
The unembodied essence, and no more
That with a quick'ning spell doth o'er us pass
As dew of the night-time, o'er the summer grass?

3

Doth o'er us pass, when, as th' expanding eye
To the lov'd object—so the tear to the lid
Will start, which lately slept in apathy?
And yet it need not be—(that object) hid
From us in life—but common—which doth lie
Each hour before us—but *then* only bid
With a strange sound, as of a harp-string broken
T' awake us—'Tis a symbol and a token.

4

Of what in other worlds shall be—and giv'n
In beauty by our God, to those alone
Who otherwise would fall from life and Heav'n
Drawn by their heart's passion, and that tone,

That high tone of the spirit which hath striv'n
Tho' not with Faith—with godliness—whose throne
With desp'rate energy 't hath beaten down;
Wearing its own deep feeling as a crown.

Israfel

In Heaven a spirit doth dwell
    "Whose heart-strings are a lute;"
None sing so wildly well
As the angel Israfel,
And the giddy stars (so legends tell)
Ceasing their hymns, attend the spell
    Of his voice, all mute.

Tottering above
    In her highest noon,
    The enamoured moon
Blushes with love,
    While, to listen, the red levin
    (With the rapid Pleiads, even,
    Which were seven,)
    Pauses in Heaven.

And they say (the starry choir
    And the other listening things)
That Israfeli's fire
Is owing to that lyre
    By which he sits and sings—
The trembling living wire
Of those unusual strings.

But the skies that angel trod,
    Where deep thoughts are a duty—
Where Love's a grown-up God—
    Where the Houri glances are
Imbued with all the beauty
    Which we worship in a star.

Therefore, thou art not wrong,
    Israfeli, who despisest
An unimpassioned song;
To thee the laurels belong,
    Best bard, because the wisest!
Merrily live, and long!

The ecstasies above
    With thy burning measures suit—
Thy grief, thy joy, thy hate, thy love,
With the fervour of thy lute—
Well may the stars be mute!

Yes, Heaven is thine; but this
    Is a world of sweets and sours;
    Our flowers are merely—flowers,
And the shadow of thy perfect bliss
    Is the sunshine of ours.

If I could dwell
Where Israfel
    Hath dwelt, and he where I,
He might not sing so wildly well
    A mortal melody,
While a bolder note than this might swell
    From my lyre within the sky.

Lenore

Ah, broken is the golden bowl!—the spirit flown forever!
Let the bell toll!—a saintly soul floats on the Stygian river:—
And, Guy De Vere, hast *thou* no tear?—weep now or never more!
See! on yon drear and rigid bier low lies thy love, Lenore!
Come, let the burial rite be read—the funeral song be sung!—
An anthem for the queenliest dead that ever died so young—
A dirge for her the doubly dead in that she died so young.

"Wretches! ye loved her for her wealth and ye hated her for her pride;
And, when she fell in feeble health, ye blessed her—that she died:—
How *shall* the ritual then be read—the requiem how be sung
By you—by yours, the evil eye—by yours the slanderous tongue
That did to death the innocence that died and died so young?

Peccavimus:—yet rave not thus! but let a Sabbath song
Go up to God so solemnly the dead may feel no wrong!
The sweet Lenore hath gone before, with Hope that flew beside,
Leaving thee wild for the dear child that should have been thy bride—
For her, the fair and debonair, that now so lowly lies,
The life upon her yellow hair, but not within her eyes—
The life still there upon her hair, the death upon her eyes.

"Avaunt!—avaunt! to friends from fiends the indignant ghost is riven—
From Hell unto a high estate within the utmost Heaven—
From moan and groan to a golden throne beside the King of Heaven:—
Let *no* bell toll, then, lest her soul, amid its hallowed mirth
Should catch the note as it doth float up from the damnéd Earth!
And I—tonight my heart is light:—no dirge will I upraise,
But waft the angel on her flight with a Pæan of old days!"

The Bells

1

Hear the sledges with the bells—
Silver bells!
What a world of merriment their melody foretells!
How they tinkle, tinkle, tinkle,
In the icy air of night!
While the stars that oversprinkle
All the Heavens, seem to twinkle
With a crystalline delight;
Keeping time, time, time,
In a sort of Runic rhyme,
To the tintinabulation that so musically wells
From the bells, bells, bells, bells,
Bells, bells, bells—
From the jingling and the tinkling of the bells.

2

Hear the mellow wedding bells—
Golden bells!
What a world of happiness their harmony foretells!
Through the balmy air of night
How they ring out their delight!—
From the molten-golden notes
And all in tune,
What a liquid ditty floats
To the turtle-dove that listens while she gloats
On the moon!
Oh, from out the sounding cells
What a gush of euphony voluminously wells!
How it swells!

How it dwells
　On the Future!—how it tells
　Of the rapture that impels
To the swinging and the ringing
　Of the bells, bells, bells!—
Of the bells, bells, bells, bells,
　　Bells, bells, bells—
To the rhyming and the chiming of the bells!

3

Hear the loud alarum bells—
　　Brazen bells!
What tale of terror, now, their turbulency tells!
　In the startled ear of Night
　How they scream out their affright!
　　Too much horrified to speak,
　　They can only shriek, shriek,
　　　Out of tune,
In a clamorous appealing to the mercy of the fire—
In a mad expostulation with the deaf and frantic fire,
　　Leaping higher, higher, higher,
　　With a desperate desire
　And a resolute endeavor
　Now—now to sit, or never,
By the side of the pale-faced moon.
　　Oh, the bells, bells, bells!
　What a tale their terror tells
　　Of despair!
　How they clang and clash and roar!
　What a horror they outpour
In the bosom of the palpitating air!
　　Yet the ear, it fully knows,

By the twanging
And the clanging,
How the danger ebbs and flows:—
Yes, the ear distinctly tells,
In the jangling
And the wrangling,
How the danger sinks and swells,
By the sinking or the swelling in the anger of the bells—
Of the bells—
Of the bells, bells, bells, bells,
Bells, bells, bells—
In the clamor and the clangor of the bells.

4

Hear the tolling of the bells—
Iron bells!
What a world of solemn thought their monody compels!
In the silence of the night
How we shiver with affright
At the melancholy meaning of the tone!
For every sound that floats
From the rust within their throats
Is a groan.
And the people—ah, the people
They that dwell up in the steeple
All alone,
And who, tolling, tolling, tolling,
In that muffled monotone,
Feel a glory in so rolling
On the human heart a stone—
They are neither man nor woman—
They are neither brute nor human,

They are Ghouls:—
And their king it is who tolls:—
And he rolls, rolls, rolls, rolls
   A Pæan from the bells!
  And his merry bosom swells
    With the Pæan of the bells!
  And he dances and he yells;
Keeping time, time, time,
In a sort of Runic rhyme,
   To the Pæan of the bells—
   Of the bells:—
Keeping time, time, time,
In a sort of Runic rhyme,
   To the throbbing of the bells—
Of the bells, bells, bells—
   To the sobbing of the bells:—
Keeping time, time, time,
   As he knells, knells, knells,
In a happy Runic rhyme,
   To the rolling of the bells—
Of the bells, bells, bells:—
   To the tolling of the bells—
Of the bells, bells, bells, bells,
   Bells, bells, bells—
To the moaning and the groaning of the bells.

Eldorado

Gaily bedight,
A gallant knight,
In sunshine and in shadow,
Had journeyed long,
Singing a song,
In search of Eldorado.

But he grew old—
This knight so bold—
And o'er his heart a shadow
Fell, as he found
No spot of ground
That looked like Eldorado.

And, as his strength
Failed him at length
He met a pilgrim shadow—
"Shadow," said he,
"Where can it be—
This land of Eldorado?"

"Over the Mountains
Of the Moon,
Down the Valley of the Shadow,
Ride, boldly ride,"
The shade replied,—
"If you seek for Eldorado!"

Margaret Fuller
1810–1850

Sistrum

Triune, shaping, restless power,
Life-flow from life's natal hour,
No music chords are in thy sound;
By some thou'rt but a rattle found;
Yet, without thy ceaseless motion,
To ice would turn their dead devotion.
Life-flow of my natal hour,
I will not weary of thy power,
Till in the changes of thy sound
A chord's three parts distinct are found.
I will faithful move with thee,
God-ordered, self-fed energy,
Nature in eternity.

Frances Sargent Osgood
1811–1850

Ah! Woman Still

Ah! woman still
  Must veil the shrine,
Where feeling feeds the fire divine,
  Nor sing at will,
  Untaught by art,
The music prison'd in her heart!
  Still gay the note,
  And light the lay,
The woodbird warbles on the spray,
  Afar to float,
  But homeward flown,
Within his nest, how changed the tone!

Oh! none can know,
  Who have not heard
The music–soul that thrills the bird,
  The carol low
  As coo of dove
He warbles to his woodland–love!
  The world would say
  'Twas vain and wild,
The impassion'd lay of Nature's child;
  And Feeling so
  Should veil the shrine
Where softly glow her fires divine!

CHRISTOPHER PEARSE CRANCH

1813-1892

Gnosis

Thought is deeper than all speech,
  Feeling deeper than all thought:
Souls to souls can never teach
  What unto themselves was taught.

We are spirits clad in veils;
  Man by man was never seen;
All our deep communing fails
  To remove the shadowy screen.

Heart to heart was never known;
  Mind with mind did never meet;
We are columns left alone
  Of a temple once complete.

Like the stars that gem the sky,
  Far apart though seeming near,
In our light we scattered lie;
  All is thus but starlight here.

What is social company
  But a babbling summer stream?
What our wise philosophy
  But the glancing of a dream?

Only when the Sun of Love
  Melts the scattered stars of thought,
Only when we live above
  What the dim-eyed world hath taught,

Only when our souls are fed
   By the Fount which gave them birth,
And by inspiration led
   Which they never drew from earth,

We, like parted drops or rain,
   Swelling till they meet and run,
Shall be all absorbed again,
   Melting, flowing into one.

December

No more the scarlet maples flash and burn
   Their beacon-fires from hilltop and from plain;
The meadow-grasses and the woodland fern
   In the bleak woods lie withered once again.

The trees stand bare, and bare each stony scar
   Upon the cliffs; half frozen glide the rills;
The steel-blue river like a scimitar
   Lies cold and curved between the dusky hills.

Over the upland farm I take my walk,
   And miss the flaunting flocks of golden-rod;
Each autumn flower a dry and leafless stalk,
   Each mossy field a track of frozen sod.

I hear no more the robin's summer song
   Through the gray network of the wintry woods;
Only the cawing crows that all day long
   Clamor about the windy solitudes.

Like agate stones upon earth's frozen breast,
   The little pools of ice lie round and still;
While sullen clouds shut downward east and west
   In marble ridges stretched from hill to hill.

Come once again, O southern wind,—once more
  Come with thy wet wings flapping at my pane;
Ere snow-drifts pile their mounds about my door,
  One parting dream of summer bring again.

Ah, no! I hear the windows rattle fast;
  I see the first flakes of the gathering snow,
That dance and whirl before the northern blast.
  No countermand the march of days can know.

December drops no weak, relenting tear,
  By our fond summer sympathies ensnared;
Nor from the perfect circle of the year
  Can even winter's crystal gems be spared.

The Pines and the Sea

Beyond the low marsh-meadows and the beach,
Seen through the hoary trunks of windy pines,
The long blue level of the ocean shines.
The distant surf, with hoarse, complaining speech,
Out from its sandy barrier seems to reach;
And while the sun behind the woods declines,
The moaning sea with sighing boughs combines,
And waves and pines make answer, each to each.
O melancholy soul, whom far and near,
In life, faith, hope, the same sad undertone
Pursues from thought to thought! thou needs must hear
An old refrain, too much, too long thine own:
'Tis thy mortality infects thine ear;
The mournful strain was in thyself alone.

JONES VERY
1813-1880

Today

I live but in the present—where art thou?
Hast thou a home in some past, future year?
I call to thee from every leafy bough,
But thou art far away and canst not hear.

Each flower lifts up its red or yellow head,
And nods to thee as thou art passing by:
Hurry not on, but stay thine anxious tread,
And thou shalt live with me, for there am I.

The stream that murmurs by thee,—heed its voice,
Nor stop thine ear; 'tis I that bid it flow;
And thou with its glad waters shalt rejoice,
And of the life I live within them know.

And hill, and grove, and flowers, and running stream,
When thou dost live with them shall look more fair;
And thou awake as from a cheating dream,
The life today with me and mine to share.

The Columbine

Still, still my eye will gaze long fixed on thee,
Till I forget that I am called a man,
And at thy side fast-rooted seem to be,
And the breeze comes my cheek with thine to fan.
Upon this craggy hill our life shall pass,
A life of summer days and summer joys,
Nodding our honey-bells mid pliant grass
In which the bee half hid his time employs;

And here we'll drink with thirsty pores the rain,
And turn dew-sprinkled to the rising sun,
And look when in the flaming west again
His orb across the heaven its path has run;
Here left in darkness on the rocky steep,
My weary eyes shall close like folding flowers in sleep.

The Morning Watch

'Tis near the morning watch, the dim lamp burns
But scarcely shows how dark the slumbering street;
No sound of life the silent mart returns;
No friends from house to house their neighbors greet;
It is the sleep of death; a deeper sleep
Than e'er before on mortal eyelids fell;
No stars above the gloom their places keep;
No faithful watchmen of the morning tell;
Yet still they slumber on, though rising day
Hath through their windows poured the awakening
    light;
Or, turning in their sluggard trances, say—
"There yet are many hours to fill the night;"
They rise not yet; while on the bridegroom goes
'Till he the day's bright gates forever on them close!

The Song

When I would sing of crooked streams and fields,
On, on from me they stretch too far and wide,
And at their look my song all powerless yields,
And down the river bears me with its tide;
Amid the fields I am a child again,
The spots that then I loved I love the more,
My fingers drop the strangely-scrawling pen,
And I remember nought but nature's lore;
I plunge me in the river's cooling wave,
Or on the embroidered bank admiring lean,
Now some endangered insect life to save,
Now watch the pictured flowers and grasses green;
Forever playing where a boy I played,
By hill and grove, by field and stream delayed.

Autumn Leaves

The leaves though thick are falling; one by one
Decayed they drop from off their parent tree;
Their work with autumn's latest day is done,
Thou see'st them borne upon its breezes free;
They lie strown here and there, their many dyes
That yesterday so caught thy passing eye;
Soiled by the rain each leaf neglected lies,
Upon the path where now thou hurriest by;
Yet think thee not their beauteous tints less fair,
Than when they hung so gaily o'er thy head;
But rather find thee eyes, and look thee there
Where now thy feet so heedless o'er them tread;
And thou shalt see where wasting now they lie,
The unseen hues of immortality.

The Earth

I would lie low, the ground on which men tread,
Swept by thy spirit like the wind of heaven;
An earth where gushing springs and corn for bread
By me at every season should be given;
Yet not the water and the bread that now
Supplies their tables with its daily food;
But Thou wouldst give me fruit for every bough,
Such as Thou givest me, and call'st it good;
And water from the stream of life should flow,
By every dwelling that thy love has built;
Whose taste the ransomed of thy son shall know,
Whose robes are washed from every stain of guilt;
And men would own it was thy hand that blest,
And from my bosom find a surer rest.

The Lost

The fairest day that ever yet has shone,
Will be when thou the day within shalt see;
The fairest rose that ever yet has blown,
When thou the flower thou lookest on shalt be.
But thou art far away among Time's toys;
Thyself the day thou lookest for in them,
Thyself the flower that now thine eye enjoys,
But wilted now thou hang'st upon thy stem.
The bird thou hearest on the budding tree,
Thou hast made sing with thy forgotten voice;
But when it swells again to melody,
The song is thine in which thou wilt rejoice;
And thou new risen 'midst these wonders live,
That now to them dost all thy substance give.

The Latter Rain

The latter rain, it falls in anxious haste
Upon the sun-dried fields and branches bare,
Loosening with searching drops the rigid waste
As if it would each root's lost strength repair;
But not a blade grows green as in the spring,
No swelling twig puts forth its thickening leaves;
The robins only mid the harvests sing
Pecking the grain that scatters from the sheaves;
The rain falls still—the fruit all ripened drops,
It pierces chestnut burr and walnut shell,
The furrowed fields disclose the yellow crops,
Each bursting pod of talents used can tell,
And all that once received the early rain
Declare to man it was not sent in vain.

The Strangers

Each care-worn face is but a book
    To tell of houses bought or sold;
Or filled with words that men have took
    From those who lived and spoke of old.

I see none whom I know, for they
    See other things than him they meet;
And though they stop me by the way,
    'Tis still some other one to greet.

There are no words that reach my ear,
    Those speak who tell of other things
Than what they mean for me to hear,
    For in their speech the counter rings.

I would be where each word is true,
  Each eye sees what it looks upon;
For here my eye has seen but few,
  Who in each act that act have done.

On Visiting the Graves of Hawthorne and Thoreau

Beneath these shades, beside you winding stream,
Lies Hawthorne's manly form, the mortal part!
The soul, that loved to meditate and dream,
Might linger here unwilling to depart,
But that a higher life has called away
To fairer scenes, to nobler work and thought.
Why should the spirit then on earth delay,
That has a glimpse of such bright regions caught!
And near another, Nature's child, doth rest,—
Thoreau, who loved each woodland path to tread;
So gently sleeping on his mother's breast!
Living, though numbered with the numerous dead.
We mourn! But hope will whisper in the heart,
We meet again! and meet no more to part.

Henry David Thoreau
1817-1862

I am a parcel of vain strivings tied

I am a parcel of vain strivings tied
   By a chance bond together,
    Dangling this way and that, their links
    Were made so loose and wide,
       Methinks,
    For milder weather.

A bunch of violets without their roots,
   And sorrel intermixed,
   Encircled by a wisp of straw
    Once coiled about their shoots,
     The law
    By which I'm fixed.

A nosegay which Time clutched from out
   Those fair Elysian fields,
   With weeds and broken stems, in haste,
    Doth make the rabble rout
     That waste
    The day he yields.

And here I bloom for a short hour unseen,
   Drinking my juices up,
   With no root in the land
    To keep my branches green,
     But stand
    In a bare cup.

Some tender buds were left upon my stem
    In mimicry of life,
  But ah! the children will not know,
    Till time has withered them,
       The woe
     With which they're rife.

But now I see I was not plucked for naught,
    And after in life's vase
  Of glass set while I might survive,
    But by a kind hand brought
      Alive
     To a strange place.

That stock thus thinned will soon redeem its hours,
    And by another year,
  Such as God knows, with freer air,
    More fruits and fairer flowers
      Will bear,
     While I droop here.

On fields oer which the reaper's hand has passd

On fields oer which the reaper's hand has passd
Lit by the harvest moon and autumn sun,
My thoughts like stubble floating in the wind
And of such fineness as October airs,
There after harvest could I glean my life
A richer harvest reaping without toil,
And weaving gorgeous fancies at my will
In subtler webs than finest summer haze.

Rumors from an Æolian Harp

There is a vale which none hath seen,
Where foot of man has never been,
Such as here lives with toil and strife,
An anxious and a sinful life.

There every virtue has its birth,
Ere it descends upon the earth,
And thither every deed returns,
Which in the generous bosom burns.

There love is warm, and youth is young,
And poetry is yet unsung,
For Virtue still adventures there,
And freely breathes her native air.

And ever, if you hearken well,
You still may hear its vesper bell,
And tread of high-souled men go by,
Their thoughts conversing with the sky.

Light-winged Smoke, Icarian Bird

Light-winged Smoke, Icarian bird;
Melting thy pinions in thy upward flight,
Lark without song, and messenger of dawn,
Circling above the hamlets as thy nest;
Or else, departing dream, and shadowy form
Of midnight vision, gathering up thy skirts;
By night star-veiling, and by day
Darkening the light and blotting out the sun;
Go thou my incense upward from this hearth,
And ask the gods to pardon this clear flame.

Inspiration

Whate'er we leave to God, God does,
　And blesses us;
The work we choose should be our own,
　God lets alone.

If with light head erect I sing,
　Though all the muses lend their force,
From my poor love of anything,
　The verse is weak and shallow as its source.

But if with bended neck I grope,
　Listening behind me for my wit,
With faith superior to hope,
　More anxious to keep back than forward it,

Making my soul accomplice there
　Unto the flame my heart hath lit,
Then will the verse forever wear,
　Time cannot bend the line which God hath writ.

Always the general show of things
　Floats in review before my mind,
And such true love and reverence brings,
　That sometimes I forget that I am blind.

But soon there comes unsought, unseen,
　Some clear divine electuary,
And I, who had but sensual been,
　Grow sensible, and as God is am wary.

I hearing get who had but ears,
　And sight who had but eyes before,
I moments live who lived but years,
　And truth discern who knew but learning's lore.

I hear beyond the range of sound,
   I see beyond the verge of sight,
New earths—and skies—and seas—around,
   And in my day the sun doth pale his light.

A clear and ancient harmony
   Pierces my soul through all the din,
As through its utmost melody,
   Further behind than they, further within.

More swift its bolt than lightning is,
   Its voice than thunder is more loud,
It doth expand my privacies
   To all, and leave me single in the crowd.

It speaks with such authority,
   With so serene and lofty tone,
That idle Time runs gadding by,
   And leaves me with Eternity alone.

Then chiefly is my natal hour,
   And only then my prime of life,
Of manhood's strength it is the flower,
   'Tis peace's end and war's beginning strife.

'T hath come in summer's broadest noon,
   By a grey wall or some chance place,
Unseasoned time, insulted June,
   And vexed the day with its presuming face.

Such fragrance round my couch it makes,
   More rich than are Arabian drugs,
That my soul scents its life, and wakes
   The body up—from 'neath its perfumed rugs.

Such is the Muse—the heavenly maid,
   The star that guides our mortal course,
Which shows where life's true kernel's laid,
   Its wheat's fine flower, and its undying force.

She with one breath attunes the spheres,
   And also my poor human heart,
With one impulse propels the years
   Around, and gives my throbbing pulse its start.

I will not doubt forever more,
   Nor falter from a steadfast faith,
For though the system be turned oer,
   God takes not back the word which once he saith.

I will then trust the love untold,
   Which not my worth nor want hath bought
Which wooed me young and woos me old,
   And call the stars to witness now my thought.

My memory I'll educate
   To know the one historic truth,
Remembering to the latest date
   The only true, and sole immortal youth.

Be but thy inspiration given,
   No matter through what dangers sought,
I'll fathom hell or climb to heaven,
   And yet esteem that cheap which love has bought.

   Fame cannot tempt the bard
      Who's famous with his God,
     Nor laurel him reward,
     Who hath his maker's nod.

Within the Circuit of This Plodding Life

Within the circuit of this plodding life
There enter moments of an azure hue,
Untarnished fair as is the violet
Or anemone, when the spring strews them
By some meandering rivulet, which make
The best philosophy untrue that aims
But to console man for his grievances.
I have remembered when the winter came,
High in my chamber in the frosty nights,
When in the still light of the cheerful moon,
On every twig and rail and jutting spout,
The icy spears were adding to their length
Against the arrows of the coming sun,
How in the shimmering noon of summer past
Some unrecorded beam slanted across
The upland pastures where the Johnswort grew;
Or heard, amid the verdure of my mind,
The bee's long smothered hum, on the blue flag
Loitering amidst the mead; or busy rill,
Which now through all its course stands still and dumb
Its own memorial,—purling at its play
Along the slopes, and through the meadows next,
Until its youthful sound was hushed at last
In the staid current of the lowland stream;
Or seen the furrows shine but late upturned,
And where the fieldfare followed in the rear,
When all the fields around lay bound and hoar
Beneath a thick integument of snow.
So by God's cheap economy made rich
To go upon my winter's task again.

My life has been the poem I would have writ

My life has been the poem I would have writ,
But I could not both live and utter it.

JULIA WARD HOWE
1819-1910

The Battle Hymn of the Republic

Mine eyes have seen the glory of the coming of the Lord:
He is trampling out the vintage where the grapes of wrath are stored;
He hath loosed the fatal lightning of His terrible swift sword:
    His truth is marching on.

I have seen Him in the watch-fires of a hundred circling camps,
They have builded Him an altar in the evening dews and damps;
I can read His righteous sentence by the dim and flaring lamps:
    His day is marching on.

I have read a fiery gospel writ in burnished rows of steel:
"As ye deal with my contemners, so with you my grace shall deal;
Let the Hero, born of woman, crush the serpent with his heel,
    Since God is marching on."

He has sounded forth the trumpet that shall never call retreat;
He is sifting out the hearts of men before His judgement seat:
Oh, be swift, my soul, to answer Him! Be jubilant, my feet!
    Our God is marching on.

In the beauty of the lilies Christ was born across the sea,
With a glory in his bosom that transfigures you and me:
As he died to make men holy, let us die to make men free,
    While God is marching on.

Middle Age

Left alone with the cows to-day,
The younger members all gone away;
The trees would go, but their roots are set,
Their patent of freedom not made out yet.
So here I sit, in state serene,
Every one's servant and no one's queen,
Watching the butterflies bright and brown,
That float like leaves from God's autumn crown.

My children are chasing the swift delight
Oft neared, but ne'er o'ertaken quite:
The sweet cup fails from the lips too soon,
The harmony waits for its perfect tune;
In bluest ether some scutcheon dark
Heralds the storm-fiend to the bark;
God's monitors set, if the sense should pall,
To whisper the spirit: "This is not all."

The grave of the Past in my garden lies
For daily and hourly sacrifice.
The Christ life blesses my daily care,
For his is the lesson and his the prayer.
But the endless Future touches me too
In the unseen Babe that, old and new,
Is carried along in the household ways
With its waiting mother, too dear for praise.

I look at the ancient blue on high
That saw the first Parents live and die,
By this very sun which, burning still,
Mirrors God's patient and constant will.
And I look below at the ancient green

Where the life of the aeons has garnered been;
There, standing where others stand between,
I study the lesson of human fate
On the wondrous page, at my narrow date.

And this later freedom, this thoughtful calm
That sobers the strophe and quickens the psalm,
That gathers the blessing and loses the pain,
And counts nought for lost in the final gain,
And the children, born without pangs of mine,
And the dreams that in young eyes dazzle and shine,
And the faith that follows the prophet's soul
Where truth unseen has its distant goal.
Let me end the song ere I turn the page,—
All this is the burthen of middle age.

JAMES RUSSELL LOWELL

1819-1891

Remembered Music

A Fragment

Thick-rushing, like an ocean vast
  Of bisons the far prairie shaking,
The notes crowd heavily and fast
As surfs, one plunging while the last
  Draws seaward from its foamy breaking.

Or in low murmurs they began,
  Rising and rising momently,
As o'er a harp Æolian
A fitful breeze, until they ran
  Up to a sudden ecstasy.

And then, like minute-drops of rain
  Ringing in water silverly,
They lingering dropped and dropped again,
Till it was almost like a pain
  To listen when the next would be.

From *The Vision of Sir Launfal*

And what is so rare as a day in June?
  Then, if ever, come perfect days;
Then Heaven tries earth if it be in tune,
  And over it softly her warm ear lays;
Whether we look, or whether we listen,
We hear life murmur, or see it glisten;
Every clod feels a stir of might,
  An instinct within it that reaches and towers,
And, groping blindly above it for light,
  Climbs to a soul in grass and flowers;

The flush of life may well be seen
   Thrilling back over hills and valleys;
The cowslip startles in meadows green,
   The buttercup catches the sun in its chalice,
And there's never a leaf nor a blade too mean
   To be some happy creature's palace;
The little bird sits at his door in the sun,
   Atilt like a blossom among the leaves,
And lets his illumined being o'errun
   With the deluge of summer it receives;
His mate feels the eggs beneath her wings,
And the heart in her dumb breast flutters and sings;
He sings to the wide world, and she to her nest,—
In the nice ear of Nature which song is the best?

To the Dandelion

   Dear common flower, that grow'st beside the way
Fringing the dusty road with harmless gold,
   First pledge of blithesome May,
Which children pluck, and, full of pride uphold,
   High-hearted buccaneers, o'erjoyed that they
An Eldorado in the grass have found
Which not the rich earth's ample round
May match in wealth, thou art more dear to me
Than all the prouder summer-blooms may be.

   Gold such as thine ne'er drew the Spanish prow
Through the primeval hush of Indian seas,
   Nor wrinkled the lean brow
Of age, to rob the lover's heart of ease;
   'Tis the Spring's largess, which she scatters now.

To rich and poor alike, with lavish hand,
Though most hearts never understand
To take it at God's value, but pass by
The offered wealth with unrewarded eye.

Thou art my tropics and mine Italy;
To look at thee unlocks a warmer clime;
The eyes thou givest me
Are in the heart, and heed not space or time:
Not in mid June the golden-cuirassed bee
Feels a more summer-like warm ravishment
In the white lily's breezy tent,
His fragrant Sybaris, than I, when first
From the dark green thy yellow circles burst.

Then think I of deep shadows on the grass,
Of meadows where in sun the cattle graze,
Where, as the breezes pass,
The gleaming rushes lean a thousand ways,
Of leaves that slumber in a cloudy mass,
Or whiten in the wind, of waters blue
That from the distance sparkle through
Some woodland gap, and of a sky above,
Where one white cloud like a stray lamb doth move.

My childhood's earliest thoughts are linked with thee;
The sight of thee calls back the robin's song,
Who, from the dark old tree
Beside the door, sang clearly all day long,
And I, secure in childish piety,
Listened as if I heard an angel sing
With news from heaven, which he could bring
Fresh every day to my untainted ears
When birds and flowers and I were happy peers.

How like a prodigal doth nature seem,
When thou, for all thy gold, so common art!
    Thou teachest me to deem
More sacredly of every human heart,
    Since each reflects in joy its scanty gleam
Of heaven, and could some wondrous secret show,
Did we but pay the love we owe,
And with a child's undoubting wisdom look
On all these living pages of God's book.

HERMAN MELVILLE
1819-1891

The Maldive Shark

About the Shark, phlegmatical one,
Pale sot of the Maldive sea,
The sleek little pilot-fish, azure and slim,
How alert in attendance be.
From his saw-pit of mouth, from his charnel of maw
They have nothing of harm to dread,
But liquidly glide on his ghastly flank
Or before his Gorgonian head;
Or lurk in the port of serrated teeth
In white triple tiers of glittering gates,
And there find a haven when peril's abroad,
An asylum in jaws of the Fates!
They are friends; and friendly they guide him to prey,
Yet never partake of the treat—
Eyes and brains to the dotard lethargic and dull,
Pale ravener of horrible meat.

The Portent

Hanging from the beam,
   Slowly swaying (such the law),
Gaunt the shadow on your green,
   Shenandoah!
The cut is on the crown
(Lo, John Brown),
And the stabs shall heal no more.

Hidden in the cap
  Is the anguish none can draw
So your future veils its face,
  Shenandoah!
But the streaming beard is shown
(Weird John Brown),
The meteor of the war.

The March into Virginia

Ending in the First Manassas
July 1861

Did all the lets and bars appear
  To every just or larger end,
Whence should come the trust and cheer?
  Youth must its ignorant impulse lend—
Age finds place in the rear.
  All wars are boyish, and are fought by boys,
The champions and enthusiasts of the state:
  Turbid ardors and vain joys
    Not barrenly abate—
Stimulants to the power mature,
  Preparatives of fate.

Who here forecasteth the event?
What heart but spurns at precedent
And warnings of the wise,
Contemned foreclosures of surprise?
The banners play, the bugles call,
The air is blue and prodigal.
  No berrying party, pleasure-wooed,
No picnic party in the May,

Ever went less loth than they
    Into that leafy neighborhood.
In Bacchic glee they file toward Fate,
Moloch's uninitiate;
Expectancy, and glad surmise
Of battle's unknown mysteries.

All they feel is this: 'tis glory,
A rapture sharp, though transitory,
Yet lasting in belaureled story.
So they gayly go to fight,
Chatting left and laughing right.

But some who this blithe mood present,
    As on in lightsome files they fare,
Shall die experienced ere three days be spent—
    Perish, enlightened by the vollied glare;
Or shame survive, and, like to adamant,
    Thy after shock, Manassas, share.

Shiloh

A Requiem
April 1862

Skimming lightly, wheeling still,
    The swallows fly low
Over the field in clouded days,
    The forest-field of Shiloh—
Over the field where April rain
Solaced the parched one stretched in pain
Through the pause of night
That followed the Sunday fight
    Around the church of Shiloh—

The church so lone, the log-built one,
That echoed to many a parting groan
   And natural prayer
Of dying foemen mingled there—
Foemen at morn, but friends at eve—
   Fame or country least their care:
(What like a bullet can undeceive!)
   But now they lie low,
While over them the swallows skim
   And all is hushed at Shiloh.

Malvern Hill

July 1862

Ye elms that wave on Malvern Hill
   In prime of morn and May,
Recall ye how McClellan's men
     Here stood at bay?
While deep within yon forest dim
   Our rigid comrades lay—
Some with the cartridge in their mouth,
Others with fixed arms lifted South—
     Invoking so
The cypress glades? Ah wilds of woe!

The spires of Richmond, late beheld
   Through rifts in musket-haze,
Were closed from view in clouds of dust
     On leaf-walled ways,
Where streamed our wagons in caravan;
   And the Seven Nights and Days

Of march and fast, retreat and fight,
Pinched our grimed faces to ghastly plight—
    Does the elm wood
Recall the haggard beards of blood?

The battle-smoked flag, with stars eclipsed,
    We followed (it never fell!)—
In silence husbanded our strength—
    Received their yell;
Till on this slope we patient turned
    With cannon ordered well;
Reverse we proved was not defeat;
But ah, the sod what thousands meet!—
    Does Malvern Wood
Bethink itself, and muse and brood?

We elms of Malvern Hill
    Remember every thing;
But sap the twig will fill;
Wag the world how it will,
    Leaves must be green in Spring.

In the Prison Pen

1864

Listless he eyes the palisades
    And sentries in the glare;
'Tis barren as a pelican-beach—
    But his world is ended there.

Nothing to do; and vacant hands
    Bring on the idiot-pain;
He tries to think—to recollect,
    But the blur is on his brain.

Around him swarm the plaining ghosts
  Like those on Virgil's shore—
A wilderness of faces dim,
  And pale ones gashed and hoar.

A smiting sun. No shed, no tree;
  He totters to his lair—
A den that sick hands dug in earth
  Ere famine wasted there,

Or, dropping in his place, he swoons,
  Walled in by throngs that press,
Till forth from the throngs they bear him dead—
  Dead in his meagreness.

"Formerly a Slave"

An Idealized Portrait, by E. Vedder, In the Spring Exhibition of the National Academy, 1865

The sufferance of her race is shown,
  And retrospect of life,
Which now too late deliverance dawns upon;
  Yet is she not at strife.

Her children's children they shall know
  The good withheld from her;
And so her reverie takes prophetic cheer—
  In spirit she sees the stir

Far down the depth of thousand years,
  And marks the revel shine;
Her dusky face is lit with sober light,
  Sibylline, yet benign.

The Berg

A Dream

I saw a ship of martial build
(Her standards set, her brave apparel on)
Directed as by madness mere
Against a stolid iceberg steer,
Nor budge it, though the infatuate ship went down.
The impact made huge ice-cubes fall
Sullen, in tons that crashed the deck;
But that one avalanche was all . . .
No other movement save the foundering wreck.

Along the spurs of ridges pale,
Not any slenderest shaft and frail,
A prism over glass-green gorges lone,
Toppled; nor lace of traceries fine,
Nor pendant drops in grot or mine
Were jarred, when the stunned ship went down.
Nor sole the gulls in cloud that wheeled
Circling one snow-flanked peak afar,
But nearer fowl the floes that skimmed
And crystal beaches, felt no jar.
No thrill transmitted stirred the lock
Of jack straw needle-ice at base;
Towers undermined by waves . . . the block
Atilt impending . . . kept their place.
Seals, dozing sleek on sliddery ledges
Slipt never, when by loftier edges
Through very inertia overthrown,
The impetuous ship in bafflement went down.

Hard Berg (methought), so cold, so vast,
With mortal damps self-overcast;
Exhaling still thy dankish breath . . .
Adrift dissolving, bound for death;
Though lumpish thou, a lumbering one . . .
A lumbering lubbard loitering slow,
Impingers rue thee and go down,
Sounding thy precipice below,
Nor stir the slimy slug that sprawls
Along thy dead indifference of walls.

Monody

To have known him, to have loved him
    After loneness long;
And then to be estranged in life,
    And neither in the wrong;
And now for death to set his seal—
    Ease me, a little ease, my song!

By wintry hills his hermit-mound
    The sheeted snow-drifts drape,
And houseless there the snow-bird flits
    Beneath the fir-trees' crape:
Glazed now with ice the cloistral vine
    That hid the shyest grape.

Art

In placid hours well pleased we dream
Of many a brave unbodied scheme.
But form to lend, pulsed life create,
What unlike things must meet and mate:
A flame to melt . . . a wind to freeze;
Sad patience . . . joyous energies;
Humility . . . yet pride and scorn;
Instinct and study; love and hate;
Audacity . . . reverence. These must mate
And fuse with Jacob's mystic heart,
To wrestle with the angel . . . Art.

WALT WHITMAN
1819-1892

Leaves of Grass (1855)

"I celebrate myself and sing myself"

I celebrate myself,
And what I assume you shall assume,
For every atom belonging to me as good belongs to you.

I loafe and invite my soul,
I lean and loafe at my ease. . . . observing a spear of summer grass.

Houses and rooms are full of perfumes. . . . the shelves are crowded
    with perfumes,
I breathe the fragrance myself, and know it and like it,
The distillation would intoxicate me also, but I shall not let it.

The atmosphere is not a perfume. . . . it has no taste of the
    distillation. . . . it is odorless,
It is for my mouth forever. . . . I am in love with it,
I will go to the bank by the wood and become undisguised and naked,
I am mad for it to be in contact with me.

The smoke of my own breath,
Echos, ripples, and buzzed whispers. . . . loveroot, silkthread, crotch and
    vine,
My respiration and inspiration. . . . the beating of my heart. . . .
    the passing of blood and air through my lungs,
The sniff of green leaves and dry leaves, and of the shore and darkcolored
    sea-rocks, and of hay in the barn,
The sound of the belched words of my voice. . . . words loosed to the
    eddies of the wind,
A few light kisses. . . . a few embraces. . . . a reaching around of arms,
The play of shine and shade on the trees as the supple boughs wag,

The delight alone or in the rush of the streets, or along the fields and
    hillsides,
The feeling of health. . . . the full-noon trill. . . . the song of me rising
    from bed and meeting the sun.

Have you reckoned a thousand acres much? Have you reckoned the earth
    much?
Have you practiced so long to learn to read?
Have you felt so proud to get at the meaning of poems?

Stop this day and night with me and you shall possess the origin of all
    poems,
You shall possess the good of the earth and sun. . . . there are millions of
    suns left,
You shall no longer take things at second or third hand. . . . nor look
    through the eyes of the dead. . . . nor feed on the spectres in books,
You shall not look through my eyes either, nor take things from me,
You shall listen to all sides and filter them from yourself.

I have heard what the talkers were talking. . . . the talk of the beginning
    and the end,
But I do not talk of the beginning or the end.

There was never any more inception than there is now,
Nor any more youth or age than there is now;
And will never be any more perfection than there is now,
Nor any more heaven or hell than there is now.

Urge and urge and urge,
Always the procreant urge of the world.

Out of the dimness opposite equals advance. . . . Always substance and
    increase,
Always a knit of identity. . . . always distinction. . . . always a breed of life.

Trippers and askers surround me,

People I meet. . . . . the effect upon me of my early life. . . . of the ward
and city I live in. . . . of the nation,

The latest news. . . . discoveries, inventories, societies. . . . authors old
and new,

My dinner, dress, associates, looks, business, compliments, dues,

The real or fancied indifference of some man or woman I love,

The sickness of one of my folks—or of myself. . . . or ill-doing. . . .
or loss or lack of money. . . . or depressions or exaltations,

They come to me days and nights and go from me again,

But they are not the Me myself.

Apart from the pulling and hauling stands what I am,

Stands amused, complacent, compassionating, idle, unitary,

Looks down, is erect, bends an arm on an impalpable certain rest,

Looks with its sidecurved head curious what will come next,

Both in and out of the game, and watching and wondering at it.

Backward I see in my own days where I sweated through fog with
linguists and contenders,

I have no mockings or arguments. . . . I witness and wait.

I believe in you my soul. . . . the other I am must not abase itself to you,

And you must not be abased to the other.

Loafe with me on the grass. . . . loose the stop from your throat,

Not words, not music or rhyme I want. . . . not custom or lecture, not
even the best,

Only the lull I like, the hum of your valved voice.

A child said, What is the grass? fetching it to me with full hands;

How could I answer the child?. . . . I do not know what it is any more
than he.

I guess it must be the flag of my disposition, out of hopeful green stuff
woven.

Or I guess it is the handkerchief of the Lord,
A scented gift and remembrancer designedly dropped,
Bearing the owner's name someway in the corners, that we may see and
    remark, and say Whose?

Or I guess the grass is itself a child. . . . the produced babe of the
    vegetation.

Or I guess it is a uniform hieroglyphic,
And it means, Sprouting alike in broad zones and narrow zones,
Growing among black folks as among white,
Kanuck, Tuckahoe, Congressman, Cuff, I give them the same, I receive
    them the same.

And now it seems to me the beautiful uncut hair of graves.

Tenderly will I use you curling grass,
It may be you transpire from the breasts of young men,
It may be if I had known them I would have loved them;
It may be you are from old people and from women, and from offspring
    taken soon out of their mothers' laps,
And here you are the mothers' laps.

Twenty-eight young men bathe by the shore,
Twenty-eight young men, and all so friendly,
Twenty-eight years of womanly life, and all so lonesome.

She owns the fine house by the rise of the bank,
She hides handsome and richly drest aft the blinds of the window.

Which of the young men does she like the best?
Ah the homeliest of them is beautiful to her.

Where are you off to, lady? for I see you,
You splash in the water there, yet stay stock still in your room.

Dancing and laughing along the beach came the twenty-ninth bather,
The rest did not see her, but she saw them and loved them.

The beards of the young men glistened with wet, it ran from their
long hair,
Little streams passed all over their bodies.

An unseen hand also passed over their bodies,
It descended tremblingly from their temples and ribs.

The young men float on their backs, their white bellies swell to the sun
. . . . they do not ask who seizes fast to them,
They do not know who puffs and declines with pendant and bending
arch,
They do not think whom they souse with spray.

I am of old and young, of the foolish as much as the wise,
Regardless of others, ever regardful of others,
Maternal as well as paternal, a child as well as a man,
Stuffed with the stuff that is coarse, and stuffed with the stuff that is fine,
One of the great nation, the nation of many nations—the smallest the
same and the largest the same,
A southerner soon as a northerner, a planter nonchalant and hospitable,
A Yankee bound my own way. . . . ready for trade. . . . my joints the
limberest joints on earth and the sternest joints on earth,
A Kentuckian walking the vale of the Elkhorn in my deerskin leggings,
A boatman over the lakes or bays or along coasts. . . . a Hoosier, a Badger,
a Buckeye,
A Louisianian or Georgian, poke-easy from sandhills and pines,
At home on Canadian snowshoes or up in the bush, or with fishermen
off Newfoundland,
At home in the fleet of iceboats, sailing with the rest and tacking,
At home on the hills of Vermont or in the woods of Maine or the Texan
ranch,
Comrade of Californians. . . . comrade of free northwesterners, loving
their big proportions,
Comrade of raftsmen and coalmen—comrade of all who shake hands and
welcome to drink and meat;

A learner with the simplest, a teacher of the thoughtfulest,
A novice beginning experient of myriads of seasons,
Of every hue and trade and rank, of every caste and religion,
Not merely of the New World but of Africa Europe or Asia. . . .
    a wandering savage,
A farmer, mechanic, or artist. . . . a gentleman, sailor, lover or quaker,
A prisoner, fancy-man, rowdy, lawyer, physician or priest.

I resist anything better than my own diversity,
And breathe the air and leave plenty after me,
And am not stuck up, and am in my place.

Walt Whitman, an American, one of the roughs, a kosmos,
Disorderly fleshy and sensual. . . . eating drinking and breeding,
No sentimentalist. . . . no stander above men and women or apart from
    them. . . . no more modest than immodest.

Unscrew the locks from the doors!
Unscrew the doors themselves from their jambs!

Whoever degrades another degrades me. . . . and whatever is done or said
    returns at last to me,
And whatever I do or say I also return.

Through me the afflatus surging and surging. . . . through me the current
    and index.

I speak the password primeval. . . . I give the sign of democracy;
By God! I will accept nothing which all cannot have their counterpart of
    on the same terms.
There is that in me. . . . I do not know what it is. . . . but I know it is
    in me.

Wrenched and sweaty. . . . calm and cool then my body becomes;
I sleep. . . . I sleep long.

I do not know it. . . . it is without name. . . . it is a word unsaid,
It is not in any dictionary or utterance or symbol.

Something it swings on more than the earth I swing on,
To it the creation is the friend whose embracing awakes me.

Perhaps I might tell more. . . . Outlines! I plead for my brothers and
    sisters.

Do you see O my brothers and sisters?
It is not chaos or death. . . . it is form and union and plan. . . . it is eternal
    life. . . . it is happiness.

The past and present wilt. . . . I have filled them and emptied them,
And proceed to fill my next fold of the future.

Listener up there! Here you. . . . what have you to confide to me?
Look in my face while I snuff the sidle of evening,
Talk honestly, for no one else hears you, and I stay only a minute longer.

Do I contradict myself?
Very well then. . . . I contradict myself;
I am large. . . . I contain multitudes.

I concentrate toward them that are nigh. . . . I wait on the door-slab.

Who has done his day's work and will soonest be through with his
    supper?
Who wishes to walk with me?

Will you speak before I am gone? Will you prove already too late?

The spotted hawk swoops by and accuses me. . . . he complains of my gab
    and my loitering.

I too am not a bit tamed. . . . I too am untranslatable,
I sound my barbaric yawp over the roofs of the world.

The last scud of day holds back for me,
It flings my likeness after the rest and true as any on the shadowed wilds,
It coaxes me to the vapor and the dusk.

I depart as air. . . . I shake my white locks at the runaway sun,
I effuse my flesh in eddies and drift it in lacy jags.

I bequeath myself to the dirt to grow from the grass I love,
If you want me again look for me under your bootsoles.

You will hardly know who I am or what I mean,
But I shall be good health to you nevertheless,
And filter and fibre your blood.

Failing to fetch me at first keep encouraged,
Missing me one place search another,
I stop some where waiting for you.

"There was a child went forth"

There was a child went forth every day,
And the first object he looked upon and received with wonder or pity or
    love or dread, that object he became,
And that object became part of him for the day or a certain part of the
    day . . . . or for many years or stretching cycles of years.

The early lilacs became part of this child,
And grass, and white and red morning-glories, and white and red clover,
    and the song of the phoebe-bird,
And the March-born lambs, and the sow's pink-faint litter, and the mare's
    foal, and the cow's calf, and the noisy brood of the barnyard or by the
    mire of the pond-side . . and the fish suspending themselves so
    curiously below there . . and the beautiful curious liquid . . and the
    water-plants with their graceful flat heads . . all became part of him.

And the field-sprouts of April and May became part of him. . . . winter-
grain sprouts, and those of the light-yellow corn, and of the esculent
roots of the garden,
And the appletrees covered with blossoms, and the fruit afterward. . . .
and woodberries . . and the commonest weeds by the road;
And the old drunkard staggering home from the outhouse of the tavern
whence he had lately risen,
And the schoolmistress that passed on her way to the school . . and the
friendly boys that passed . . and the quarrelsome boys . . and the tidy
and freshcheeked girls . . and the barefoot negro boy and girl,
And all the changes of city and country wherever he went.
His own parents . . he that had propelled the fatherstuff at night, and
fathered him . . and she that conceived him in her womb and birthed
him. . . . they gave this child more of themselves than that,
They gave him afterward every day. . . . they and of them became part of
him.

The mother at home quietly placing the dishes on the suppertable,
The mother with mild words. . . . clean her cap and gown . . . . a whole-
some odor falling off her person and clothes as she walks by,
The father, strong, selfsufficient, manly, mean, angered, unjust,
The blow, the quick loud word, the tight bargain, the crafty lure,
The family usages, the language, the company, the furniture. . . . the
yearning and swelling heart,
Affection that will not be gainsayed. . . . The sense of what is real. . . .
the thought if after all it should prove unreal,
The doubts of daytime and the doubts of nighttime . . . the curious
whether and how,
Whether that which appears so is so. . . . Or is it all flashes and specks?
Men and women crowding fast in the streets . . if they are not flashes and
specks what are they?
The streets themselves, and the facades of houses. . . . the goods in the
windows,

Vehicles . . teams . . the tiered wharves, and the huge crossing at the
    ferries;
The village on the highland seen from afar at sunset . . . the river
    between,
Shadows . . aureola and mist . . light falling on roofs and gables of white
    or brown, three miles off,
The schooner near by sleepily dropping down the tide . . the little boat
    slacktowed astern,
The hurrying tumbling waves and quickbroken crests and slapping;
The strata of colored clouds. . . . the long bar of maroontint away solitary
    by itself. . . . the spread of purity it lies motionless in,
The horizon's edge, the flying seacrow, the fragrance of saltmarsh and
    shoremud;
These became part of that child who went forth every day, and who now
    goes and will always go forth every day,
And these become of him or her that peruses them now.

ALICE CARY
1820-1871

To Solitude

I am weary of the working.
Weary of the long day's heat;
To thy comfortable bosom,
Wilt thou take me, spirit sweet?

Weary of the long, blind struggle
For a pathway bright and high,—
Weary of the dimly dying
Hopes that never quite all die.

Weary searching a bad cipher
For a good that must be meant;
Discontent with being weary,—
Weary with my discontent.

I am weary of the trusting
Where my trusts but torments prove:
Wilt thou keep faith with me? wilt thou
Be my true and tender love?

I am weary drifting, driving
Like a helmless bark at sea;
Kindly, comfortable spirit,
Wilt thou give thyself to me?

Give thy birds to sing me sonnets?
Give thy winds my cheeks to kiss?
And thy mossy rocks to stand for
The memorials of our bliss?

I in reverence will hold thee,
Never vexed with jealous ills,
Though thy wild and wimpling waters
Wind about a thousand hills.

FREDERICK GODDARD TUCKERMAN
1821-1873

Sonnet

The starry flower, the flower-like stars that fade
And brighten with the daylight and the dark,—
The bluet in the green I faintly mark,
And glimmering crags with laurel overlaid,
Even to the Lord of light, the Lamp of shade,
Shine one to me,—the least, still glorious made
As crownèd moon, or heaven's great hierarch.
And, so, dim grassy flower, and night-lit spark,
Still move me on and upward for the True;
Seeking through change, growth, death, in new and old.
The full in few, the statelier in the less,
With patient pain; always remembering this,—
His hand, who touched the sod with showers of gold,
Stippled Orion on the midnight blue.

THOMAS WENTWORTH HIGGINSON
1823-1911

Decoration

Mid the flower-wreathed tombs I stand
Bearing lilies in my hand.
Comrades! in what soldier-grave
Sleeps the bravest of the brave?

Is it he who sank to rest
With his colors round his breast?
Friendship makes his tomb a shrine;
Garlands veil it: ask not mine.

One low grave, yon trees beneath,
Bears no roses, wears no wreath;
Yet no heart more high and warm
Ever dared the battle-storm,

Never gleamed a prouder eye
In the front of victory,
Never foot had firmer tread
On the field where hope lay dead,

Than are hid within this tomb,
Where the untended grasses bloom,
And no stone, with feigned distress,
Mocks the sacred loneliness.

Youth and beauty, dauntless will,
Dreams that life could ne'er fulfil,
Here lie buried; here in peace
Wrongs and woes have found release.

Turning from my comrades' eyes,
Kneeling where a woman lies,
I strew lilies on the grave
Of the bravest of the brave.

To Duty

Light of dim mornings, shield from heat and cold;
Balm for all ailments; substitute for praise;
Comrade of those who plod in lonely ways
(Ways that grow lonelier as the years wax old);
Tonic for fears; check to the over-bold;
Nurse, whose calm hand its strong restriction lays,
Kind but resistless, on our wayward days;
Mart, where high wisdom at vast price is sold;
Gardener, whose touch bids the rose-petals fall,
The thorns endure; surgeon, who human hearts
Searchest with probes, though the death-touch be given;
Spell that knits friends, but yearning lovers parts;
Tyrant relentless o'er our blisses all;—
Oh, can it be, thine other name is Heaven?

Phoebe Cary
1824-1871

Nearer Home

One sweetly solemn thought
   Comes to me o'er and o'er;
I am nearer home to-day
   Than I ever have been before;

Nearer my Father's house,
   Where the many mansions be;
Nearer the great white throne,
   Nearer the crystal sea;

Nearer the bound of life,
   Where we lay our burdens down;
Nearer leaving the cross,
   Nearer gaining the crown!

But lying darkly between,
   Winding down through the night,
Is the silent, unknown stream,
   That leads at last to the light.

Closer and closer my steps
   Come to the dread abysm:
Closer Death to my lips
   Presses the awful chrism.

Oh, if my mortal feet
   Have almost gained the brink;
If it be I am nearer home
   Even to-day than I think;

Father, perfect my trust;
   Let my spirit feel in death,
That her feet are firmly set
   On the rock of a living faith!

STEPHEN COLLINS FOSTER

1826–1864

My Old Kentucky Home

The sun shines bright in the old Kentucky home;
   'Tis summer, the darkeys are gay;
The corn-top's ripe, and the meadow's in the bloom,
   While the birds make music all the day.

The young folks roll on the little cabin floor,
   All merry, all happy and bright;
By-'n'-by hard times comes a-knocking at the door:—
   Then my old Kentucky home, good-night!

   Weep no more, my lady,
   O, weep no more to-day!
We will sing one song for the old Kentucky home,
   For the old Kentucky home, far away.

They hunt no more for the possum and the coon,
   On the meadow, the hill, and the shore;
They sing no more by the glimmer of the moon,
   On the bench by the old cabin door.
The day goes by like a shadow o'er the heart,
   With sorrow, where all was delight;
The time has come when the darkeys have to part:—
   Then my old Kentucky home, good-night!

The head must bow, and the back will have to bend,
   Wherever the darkey may go;
A few more days, and the trouble all will end,
   In the field where the sugar-canes grow.
A few more days for to tote the weary load,—
   No matter, 'twill never be light;
A few more days till we totter on the road:—
   Then my old Kentucky home, good-night!

Weep no more, my lady,
O, weep no more to-day!
We will sing one song for the old Kentucky home,
For the old Kentucky home, far away.

LUCY LARCOM
1826-1893

A Strip of Blue

I do not own an inch of land,
    But all I see is mine,—
The orchard and the mowing-fields,
    The lawns and gardens fine.
The winds my tax-collectors are,
    They bring me tithes divine,—
Wild scents and subtle essences,
    A tribute rare and free;
And, more magnificent than all,
    My window keeps for me
A glimpse of blue immensity,—
    A little strip of sea.

Richer am I than he who owns
    Great fleets and argosies;
I have a share in every ship
    Won by the inland breeze,
To loiter on yon airy road
    Above the apple-trees,
I freight them with my untold dreams;
    Each bears my own picked crew;
And nobler cargoes wait for them
    Than ever India knew,—
My ships that sail into the East
    Across that outlet blue.

Sometimes they seem like living shapes,—
    The people of the sky,—
Guests in white raiment coming down
    From heaven, which is close by;

I call them by familiar names,
  As one by one draws nigh.
So white, so light, so spirit-like,
  From violet mists they bloom!
The aching wastes of the unknown
  Are half reclaimed from gloom,
Since on life's hospitable sea
  All souls find sailing-room.

The ocean grows a weariness
  With nothing else in sight;
Its east and west, its north and south,
  Spread out from morn till night;
We miss the warm, caressing shore,
  Its brooding shade and light.

HENRY TIMROD

1829-1867

At Magnolia Cemetery

Sleep sweetly in your humble graves,
    Sleep, martyrs of a fallen cause;
Though yet no marble column craves
    The pilgrim here to pause.

In seeds of laurel in the earth
    The blossom of your fame is blown,
And somewhere, waiting for its birth,
    The shaft is in the stone!

Meanwhile, behalf the tardy years
    Which keep in trust your storied tombs,
Behold! your sisters bring their tears,
    And these memorial blooms.

Small tributes! but your shades will smile
    More proudly on these wreaths to-day,
Than when some cannon-moulded pile
    Shall overlook this bay.

Stoop, angels, hither from the skies!
    There is no holier spot of ground
Than where defeated valor lies,
    By mourning beauty crowned.

Quatorzain

Most men know love but as a part of life;
They hide it in some corner of the breast,
Even from themselves; and only when they rest
In the brief pauses of that daily strife,
Wherewith the world might else be not so rife,

They draw it forth (as one draws forth a toy
To soothe some ardent, kiss-exacting boy)
And hold it up to sister, child, or wife.
Ah me! why may not love and life be one?
Why walk we thus alone, when by our side,
Love, like a visible god, might be our guide?
How would the marts grow noble! and the street,
Worn like a dungeon-floor by weary feet,
Seem then a golden court-way of the Sun!

Charleston

Calm as that second summer which precedes
    The first fall of the snow,
In the broad sunlight of heroic deeds,
    The city bides the foe.

As yet, behind their ramparts, stern and proud,
    Her bolted thunders sleep,—
Dark Sumter, like a battlemented cloud,
    Looms o'er the solemn deep.

No Calpe frowns from lofty cliff or scaur
    To guard the holy strand;
But Moultric holds in leash her dogs of war
    Above the level sand.

And down the dunes a thousand guns lie couched,
    Unseen, beside the flood,—
Like tigers in some Orient jungle crouched,
    That wait and watch for blood.

Meanwhile, through streets still echoing with trade,
    Walk grave and thoughtful men,
Whose hands may one day wield the patriot's blade
    As lightly as the pen.

And maidens, with such eyes as would grow dim
   Over a bleeding hound,
Seem each one to have caught the strength of him
   Whose sword she sadly bound.

Thus girt without and garrisoned at home,
   Day patient following day,
Old Charleston looks from roof and spire and dome,
   Across her tranquil bay.

Ships, through a hundred foes, from Saxon lands
   And spicy Indian ports,
Bring Saxon steel and iron to her hands,
   And summer to her courts.

But still, along yon dim Atlantic line,
   The only hostile smoke
Creeps like a harmless mist above the brine,
   From some frail floating oak.

Shall the spring dawn, and she, still clad in smiles,
   And with an unscathed brow,
Rest in the strong arms of her palm-crowned isles,
   As fair and free as now?

We know not; in the temple of the Fates
   God has inscribed her doom:
And, all untroubled in her faith, she waits
   The triumph or the tomb.

EMILY DICKINSON
1830-1886

Success Is Counted Sweetest

Success is counted sweetest
By those who ne'er succeed.
To comprehend a nectar
Requires sorest need.

Not one of all the purple host
Who took the flag to-day
Can tell the definition,
So clear, of victory,

As he, defeated, dying,
On whose forbidden ear
The distant strains of triumph
Break, agonized and clear.

The Soul Selects Her Own Society

The soul selects her own society,
Then shuts the door;
On her divine majority
Obtrude no more.

Unmoved, she notes the chariot's pausing
At her low gate;
Unmoved, an emperor is kneeling
Upon her mat.

I've known her from an ample nation
Choose one;
Then close the valves of her attention
Like stone.

Much Madness Is Divinest Sense

Much madness is divinest sense
To a discerning eye;
Much sense the starkest madness.
'Tis the majority
In this, as all, prevails.
Assent, and you are sane;
Demur,—you're straightway dangerous,
And handled with a chain.

I'll Tell You How the Sun Rose

I'll tell you how the sun rose,—
A ribbon at a time.
The steeples swam in amethyst,
The news like squirrels ran.

The hills untied their bonnets,
The bobolinks begun.
Then I said softly to myself,
"That must have been the sun!"

. . .

But how he set, I know not.
There seemed a purple stile
Which little yellow boys and girls
Were climbing all the while

Till when they reached the other side,
A dominic in gray
Put gently up the evening bars,
And led the flock away.

There's a Certain Slant of Light

There's a certain slant of light,
On winter afternoons,
That oppresses, like the weight
Of cathedral tunes.

Heavenly hurt it gives us;
We can find no scar,
But internal difference
Where the meanings are.

None may teach it anything,
'Tis the seal, despair,—
An imperial affliction
Sent us of the air.

When it comes, the landscape listens,
Shadows hold their breath;
When it goes, 'tis like the distance
On the look of death.

If You Were Coming in the Fall

If you were coming in the fall,
I'd brush the summer by
With half a smile and half a spurn,
As housewives do a fly.

If I could see you in a year,
I'd wind the months in balls,
And put them each in separate drawers,
Until their time befalls.

If only centuries delayed,
I'd count them on my hand,
Subtracting till my fingers dropped
Into Van Diemen's land.

If certain, when this life was out,
That yours and mine should be,
I'd toss it yonder like a rind,
And taste eternity.

But now, all ignorant of the length
Of time's uncertain wing,
It goads me, like the goblin bee,
That will not state its sting.

A Wounded Deer Leaps Highest

A wounded deer leaps highest,
I've heard the hunter tell;
'Tis but the ecstasy of death,
And then the brake is still.

The smitten rock that gushes,
The trampled steel that springs:
A cheek is always redder
Just where the hectic stings!

Mirth is the mail of anguish,
In which it cautions arm,
Lest anybody spy the blood
And "You're hurt" exclaim!

Pain Has an Element of Blank

Pain has an element of blank;
It cannot recollect
When it began, or if there were
A day when it was not.

It has no future but itself,
Its infinite realms contain
Its past, enlightened to perceive
New periods of pain.

I Died for Beauty

I died for beauty, but was scarce
Adjusted in the tomb,
When one who died for truth was lain
In an adjoining room.

He questioned softly why I failed?
"For beauty," I replied.
"And I for truth,—the two are one;
We brethren are," he said.

And so, as kinsmen met a night,
We talked between the rooms,
Until the moss had reached our lips,
And covered up our names.

Safe in Their Alabaster Chambers

Safe in their alabaster chambers,
Untouched by morning and untouched by noon,
Sleep the meek members of the resurrection,
Rafter of satin, and roof of stone.

Light laughs the breeze in her castle of sunshine;
Babbles the bee in a stolid ear;
Pipe the sweet birds in ignorant cadence,—
Ah, what sagacity perished here!

Grand go the years in the crescent above them;
Worlds scoop their arcs, and firmaments row,
Diadems drop and Doges surrender,
Soundless as dots on a disk of snow.

Because I Could Not Stop for Death

Because I could not stop for Death,
He kindly stopped for me;
The carriage held but just ourselves
And Immortality.

We slowly drove, he knew no haste,
And I had put away
My labor, and my leisure too,
For his civility.

We passed the school where children played,
Their lessons scarcely done;
We passed the fields of gazing grain,
We passed the setting sun.

We paused before a house that seemed
A swelling of the ground;
The roof was scarcely visible,
The cornice but a mound.

Since then 'tis centuries; but each
Feels shorter than the day
I first surmised the horses' heads
Were toward eternity.

Hope Is the Thing with Feathers

Hope is the thing with feathers
That perches in the soul,
And sings the tune without the words,
And never stops at all,

And sweetest in the gale is heard;
And sore must be the storm
That could abash the little bird
That kept so many warm.

I've heard it in the chillest land,
And on the strangest sea;
Yet, never, in extremity,
It asked a crumb of me.

I'm Nobody! Who Are You?

I'm nobody! Who are you?
Are you nobody, too?
Then there's a pair of us—don't tell!
They'd banish us, you know.

How dreary to be somebody!
How public, like a frog
To tell your name the livelong day
To an admiring bog!

Just Lost When I Was Saved!

Just lost when I was saved!
Just felt the world go by!
Just girt me for the onset with eternity,
When breath blew back,
And on the other side
I heard recede the disappointed tide!

Therefore, as one returned, I feel,
Odd secrets of the line to tell!
Some sailor, skirting foreign shores,
Some pale reporter from the awful doors
Before the seal!

Next time, to stay!
Next time, the things to see
By ear unheard,
Unscrutinized by eye.

Next time, to tarry,
While the ages steal,—
Slow tramp the centuries,
And the cycles wheel.

I Cannot Live with You

I cannot live with you
It would be life,
And life is over there
Behind the shelf

The sexton keeps the key to,
Putting up
Our life, his porcelain,
Like a cup

Discarded of the housewife,
Quaint or broken;
A newer Sèvres pleases,
Old ones crack.

I could not die with you,
For one must wait
To shut the other's gaze down,—
You could not.

And I, could I stand by
And see you freeze,
Without my right of frost,
Death's privilege?

Nor could I rise with you,
Because your face
Would put out Jesus',
That new grace

Glow plain and foreign
On my homesick eye,
Except that you, than he
Shone closer by.

They'd judge us—how?
For you served Heaven, you know,
Or sought to;
I could not,

Because you saturated sight,
And I had no more eyes
For sordid excellence
As Paradise.

And were you lost, I would be,
Though my name
Rang loudest
On the heavenly fame.

And were you saved,
And I condemned to be
Where you were not,
That self were hell to me.

So we must keep apart,
You there, I here,
With just the door ajar
That oceans are,
And prayer,
And that pale sustenance,
Despair!

Wild Nights! Wild Nights!

Wild nights! Wild nights!
Were I with thee,
Wild nights should be
Our luxury!

Futile the winds
To a heart in port,—
Done with the compass,
Done with the chart.

Rowing in Eden!
Ah! the sea!
Might I but moor
Tonight in thee!

I Heard a Fly Buzz When I Died

I heard a fly buzz when I died;
    The stillness round my form
Was like the stillness in the air
    Between the heaves of storm.

The eyes beside had wrung them dry,
    And breaths were gathering sure
For that last onset, when the king
    Be witnessed in his power.

I willed my keepsakes, signed away
    What portion of me I
Could make assignable,—and then
    There interposed a fly,

With blue, uncertain, stumbling buzz,
   Between the light and me;
And then the windows failed, and then
   I could not see to see.

The Props Assist the House

The props assist the house
Until the house is built,
And then the props withdraw—
And adequate, erect,
The house supports itself;
Ceasing to recollect
The auger and the carpenter.
Just such a retrospect
Hath the perfected life,
A past of plank and nail,
And slowness,—then the scaffolds drop—
Affirming it a soul.

HELEN HUNT JACKSON
1830-1885

Poppies on the Wheat

Along Ancona's hills the shimmering heat,
A tropic tide of air with ebb and flow
Bathes all the fields of wheat until they glow
Like flashing seas of green, which toss and beat
Around the vines. The poppies lithe and fleet
Seem running, fiery torchmen, to and fro
To mark the shore.
                The farmer does not know
That they are there. He walks with heavy feet,
Counting the bread and wine by autumn's gain,
But I,—I smile to think that days remain
Perhaps to me in which, though bread be sweet
No more, and red wine warm my blood in vain,
I shall be glad remembering how the fleet,
Lithe poppies ran like torchmen with the wheat.

Two Truths

'Darling,' he said, 'I never meant
   To hurt you;' and his eyes were wet.
'I would not hurt you for the world:
   Am I to blame if I forget?'

'Forgive my selfish tears' she cried,
   'Forgive! I knew that it was not
Because you meant to hurt me, sweet—
   I knew it was that you forgot!'

But all the same, deep in her heart
    Rankled this thought, and rankles yet,—
'When love is at its best, one loves
    So much that he cannot forget.'

Emigravit

With sails full set, the ship her anchor weighs.
Strange names shines out beneath her figure head.
What glad farewells with eager eyes are said!
What cheer for him who goes, and him who stays!
Fair skies, rich lands, new homes, and untried days
Some go to seek: the rest but wait instead,
Watching the way wherein their comrades led,
Until the next stanch ship her flag doth raise.
Who knows what myriad colonies there are
Of fairest fields, and rich, undreamed-of gains
Thick planted in the distant shining plains
Which we call sky because they lie so far?
Oh, write of me, not "Died in bitter pains,"
But "Emigrated to another star!"

My Lighthouses

At westward window of a palace gray,
Which its own secret still so safely keeps
That no man now its builder's name can say,
I lie and idly sun myself to-day,
Dreaming awake far more than one who sleeps,
Serenely glad, although my gladness weeps.

I look across the harbor's misty blue,
And find and lose that magic shifting line
Where sky one shade less blue meets sea, and through
The air I catch one flush as if it knew
Some secret of that meeting, which no sign
Can show to eyes so far and dim as mine.

More ships than I can count build mast by mast
Gay lattice-work with waving green and red
Across my window-panes. The voyage past,
They crowd to anchorage so glad, so fast,
Gliding like ghosts, with noiseless breath and tread,
Mooring like ghosts, with noiseless iron and lead.

"O ships and patient men who fare by sea,"
I stretch my hands and vainly questioning cry,
"Sailed ye from west? How many nights could ye
Tell by the lights just where my dear and free
And lovely land lay sleeping? Passed ye by
Some danger safe, because her fires were nigh?"

Ah me! my selfish yearning thoughts forget
How darkness but a hand's-breadth from the coast
With danger in an evil league is set!
Ah! helpless ships and men more helpless yet,
Who trust the land-lights' short and empty boast;
The lights ye bear aloft and prayers avail ye most.

But I—ah, patient men who fare by sea,
Ye would but smile to hear this empty speech,—
I have such beacon-lights to burn for me,
In that dear west so lovely, new, and free,
That evil league by day, by night, can teach
No spell whose harm my little bark can reach.

No towers of stone uphold those beacon-lights;
No distance hides them, and no storm can shake;
In valleys they light up the darkest nights,
They outshine sunny days on sunny heights;
They blaze from every house where sleep or wake
My own who love me for my own poor sake.

Each thought they think of me lights road of flame
Across the seas; no travel on it tires
My heart. I go if they but speak my name;
From Heaven I should come and go the same,
And find this glow forestalling my desires.
My darlings, do you hear me? Trim the fires!

Her Eyes

That they are brown, no man will dare to say
He knows. And yet I think that no man's look
Ever those depths of light and shade forsook,
Until their gentle pain warned him away.
Of all sweet things I know but one which may
Be likened to her eyes.
                        When, in deep nook
Of some green field, the water of a brook
Makes lingering, whirling eddy in its way,
Round soft drowned leaves; and in a flash of sun
They turn to gold, until the ripples run
Now brown, now yellow, changing as by some
Swift spell.
            I know not with what body come
The saints. But this I know, my Paradise
Will mean the resurrection of her eyes.

Memoir of a Queen

Her name, before she was a queen, boots not.
When she was crowned, her kingdom said, "The
    Queen!"
And, after that, all other names too mean
By far had seemed. Perhaps all were forgot,
Save "Queen, sweet queen."
                  Such pitiable lot
As till her birth her kingdom had, was seen
Never in all fair lands, so torn between
False grasping powers, that toiled and fought, but got
No peace.
          All curious search is wholly vain
For written page or stone whereon occurs
A mention of the kingdom which obeyed
This sweet queen's rule. But centuries have laid
No dead queen down in royal sepulchres
Whose reign was greater or more blest than hers.

Covert

One day, when sunny fields lay warm and still,
    And from their tufted hillocks, thick and sweet
    With moss and pine and ferns, such spicy heat
Rose up, it seemed the air to overfill,
And quicken every sense with subtle thrill,
    I rambled on with careless, aimless feet,
    And lingered idly, finding all so sweet.

Sudden, almost beneath my footsteps' weight,
   Almost before the sunny silence heard
   Their sound, from a low bush, which scarcely stirred
A twig at lightening of its hidden freight,
Flew, frightened from her nest, the small brown mate
   Of some melodious, joyous, soaring bird,
   Whose song that instant high in air I heard.

     . . .

"Ah! Heart," I said, "when days are warm and sweet,
   And sunny hours for very joy are still,
   And every sense feels subtle, languid thrill
Of voiceless memory's renewing heat,
Fly not at sound of strangers' aimless feet!
   Of thy love's distant song drink all thy fill!
   Thy hiding-place is safe. Glad heart, keep still!"

THOMAS BAILEY ALDRICH
1836-1907

Memory

My mind lets go a thousand things,
Like dates of wars and deaths of kings,
And yet recalls the very hour—
'T was noon by yonder village tower,
And on the last blue noon in May—
The wind came briskly up this way,
Crisping the brook beside the road;
Then, pausing here, set down its load
Of pine-scents, and shook listlessly
Two petals from that wild-rose tree.

WILLIAM DEAN HOWELLS
1837–1920

Change

Sometimes, when after spirited debate
Of letters or affairs, in thought I go
Smiling unto myself, and all aglow
With some immediate purpose, and elate
As if my little, trivial scheme were great,
And what I would so were already so:
Suddenly I think of her that died, and know,
Whatever friendly or unfriendly fate
Befall me in my hope or in my pride,
It is all nothing but a mockery,
And nothing can be what it used to be,
When I could bid my happy life abide,
And build on earth for perpetuity,
Then, in the deathless days before she died.

Hope

We sailed and sailed upon the desert sea
Where for whole days we alone seemed to be.
At last we saw a dim, vague line arise
Between the empty billows and the skies,
That grew and grew until it wore the shape
Of cove and inlet, promontory and cape;
Then hills and valleys, rivers, fields, and woods,
Steeples and roofs, and village neighborhoods.
And then I thought, "Sometime I shall embark
Upon a sea more desert and more dark
Than ever this was, and between the skies
And empty billows I shall see arise
Another world out of that waste and lapse,
Like yonder land. Perhaps—perhaps—perhaps!"

SIDNEY LANIER
1842-1881

A Ballad of Trees and the Master

Into the woods my Master went,
Clean forspent, forspent.
Into the woods my Master came,
Forspent with love and shame.
But the olives they were not blind to Him;
The little gray leaves were kind to Him;
The thorn-tree had a mind to Him
When into the woods He came.

Out of the woods my Master went,
And He was well content.
Out of the woods my Master came,
Content with death and shame.
When Death and Shame would woo Him last,
From under the trees they drew Him last:
'Twas on a tree they slew Him—last,
When out of the woods He came.

Opposition

Of fret, of dark, of thorn, of chill,
    Complain no more; for these, O heart,
Direct the random of the will
    As rhymes direct the rage of art.

The lute's fixt fret, that runs athwart
    The strain and purpose of the string,
For governance and nice consort
    Doth bar his wilful wavering.

The dark hath many dear avails;
   The dark distils divinest dews;
The dark is rich with nightingales,
   With dreams, and with the heavenly Muse.

Bleeding with thorns of petty strife,
   I'll ease (as lovers do) my smart
With sonnets to my lady Life
   Writ red in issues from the heart.

What grace may lie within the chill
   Of favor frozen fast in scorn!
When Good's a-freeze, we call it Ill!
   This rosy Time is glacier-born.

Of fret, of dark, of thorn, of chill,
   Complain thou not, O heart; for these
Bank in the current of the will
   To uses, arts, and charities.

Clover

Inscribed to the Memory of John Keats

Dear uplands, Chester's favorable fields,
My large unjealous Loves, many yet one—
A grave good-morrow to your Graces, all,
Fair tilth and fruitful seasons!
                Lo, how still
The midmorn empties you of men, save me;
Speak to your lover, meadows! None can hear.
I lie as lies yon placid Brandywine,
Holding the hills and heavens in my heart
For contemplation.
            'Tis a perfect hour.
From founts of dawn the fluent autumn day
Has rippled as a brook right pleasantly

Half-way to noon; but now with widening turn
Makes pause, in lucent meditation locked,
And rounds into a silver pool of morn,
Bottom'd with clover-fields. My heart just hears
Eight lingering strokes of some far village-bell,
That speak the hour so inward-voiced, meseems
Time's conscience has but whispered him eight hints
Of revolution. Reigns that mild surcease
That stills the middle of each rural morn—
When nimble noises that with sunrise ran
About the farms have sunk again to rest;
When Tom no more across the horse-lot calls
To sleepy Dick, nor Dick husk-voiced upbraids
The sway-back'd roan for stamping on his foot
With sulphurous oath and kick in flank, what time
The cart-chain clinks across the slanting shaft,
And, kitchenward, the rattling bucket plumps
Souse down the well, where quivering ducks quack loud,
And Susan Cook is singing.
And burned, and loved, and ached with public shame,
And found no friends to breathe their loves to, save
Woods and wet pillows? This was all? This Ox?
"Nay," quoth a sum of voices in mine ear,
"God's clover, we, and feed His Course-of-things;
The pasture is God's pasture; systems strange
Of food and fiberment He hath, whereby
The general brawn is built for plans of His
To quality precise. Kinsman, learn this:
The artist's market is the heart of man;
The artist's price, some little good of man.
Tease not thy vision with vain search for ends.
The End of Means is art that works by love.
The End of Ends . . . in God's Beginning's lost."

JOAQUIN MILLER
1841-1913

At the Grave of Walker

He lies low in the levelled sand,
Unsheltered from the tropic sun,
And now of all he knew not one
Will speak him fair in that far land.
Perhaps 'twas this that made me seek,
Disguised, his grave one winter-tide;
A weakness for the weaker side,
A siding with the helpless weak.

A palm not far held out a hand,
Hard by a long green bamboo swung,
And bent like some great bow unstrung,
And quivered like a willow wand;
Perched on its fruits that crooked hang,
Beneath a broad banana's leaf,
A bird in rainbow splendor sang
A low, sad song, of tempered grief.

No sod, no sign, no cross nor stone,
But at his side a cactus green
Upheld its lances long and keen;
It stood in sacred sands alone,
Flat-palmed and fierce with lifted spears;
One bloom of crimson crowned its head,
A drop of blood, so bright, so red,
Yet redolent as roses' tears.

In my left hand I held a shell,
All rosy lipped and pearly red;
I laid it by his lowly bed,
For he did love so passing well
The grand songs of the solemn sea.
O shell! sing well, wild, with a will,
When storms blow loud and birds be still,
The wildest sea-song known to thee!

I said some things with folded hands,
Soft whispered in the dim sea-sound,
And eyes held humbly to the ground,
And frail knees sunken in the sands.
He had done more than this for me,
And yet I could not well do more:
I turned me down the olive shore,
And set a sad face to the sea.

Crossing the Plains

What great yoked brutes with briskets low,
With wrinkled necks like buffalo,
With round, brown, liquid, pleading eyes,
That turned so slow and sad to you,
That shone like love's eyes soft with tears,
That seemed to plead, and make replies,
The while they bowed their necks and drew
The creaking load; and looked at you.
Their sable briskets swept the ground,
Their cloven feet kept solemn sound.

Two sullen bullocks led the line,
Their great eyes shining bright like wine;
Two sullen captive kings were they,
That had in time held herds at bay,
And even now they crushed the sod
With stolid sense of majesty,
And stately stepped and stately trod,
As if 't were something still to be
Kings even in captivity.

AMBROSE BIERCE
1842-1914?

Montefiore

I saw—'twas in a dream, the other night—
A man whose hair with age was thin and white;
    One hundred years had bettered by his birth,
And still his step was firm, his eye was bright.

Before him and about him pressed a crowd.
Each head in reverence was bared and bowed,
    And Jews and Gentiles in a hundred tongues
Extolled his deeds and spake his fame aloud.

I joined the throng and, pushing forward, cried,
"Montefiore!" with the rest, and vied
    In efforts to caress the hand that ne'er
To want and worth had charity denied.

So closely round him swarmed our shouting clan
He scarce could breathe, and, taking from a pan
    A gleaming coin, he tossed it o'er our heads,
And in a moment was a lonely man!

JOHN BANISTER TABB
1845-1909

Evolution

Out of the dusk a shadow,
    Then, a spark;
Out of the cloud a silence,
    Then, a lark;
Out of the heart a rapture,
    Then, a pain;
Out of the dead, cold ashes,
    Life again.

Anonymous

Anonymous—nor needs a name
To tell the secret whence the flame,
With light, and warmth, and incense, came
A new creation to proclaim.

So was it when, His labor done,
God saw His work, and smiled thereon:
His glory in the picture shone,
But name upon the canvas, none.

LILLA CABOT PERRY
1848-1933

Meeting After Long Absence

I
As she feared it would be

Here in this room where first we met,
  And where we said farewell with tears,
Here, where you swore "Though you forget,
  My love shall deeper grow with years,"

Here, where the pictures on the wall,
  The very rugs upon the floor,
The smallest objects you recall,—
  I am awaiting you once more.

The books that we together read,—
  From off their shelves they beckon me,
All here seems living! What is dead?
  What is the ghost I fear to see?

Unchanged am I. Did you despise
  My love as "small"?—it fills my heart!
You come—a stranger from your eyes
  Looks out—and, meeting, first we part.

II
As it was

I told myself in singing words
  That you were changed and I was true;
I would not trust winds, waves, and birds
  That change was not in you.

I sang Love's dirge before we met,—
　"As murdered corpse in river bed
In eyes my heart cannot forget
　I see Love lying dead!"

You came—one look—no word was spoken,
　Our hands, once clasped, forgot to part,
And, though our silence is unbroken,
　Heart has found rest on heart.

SARAH ORNE JEWETT
1849-1887

At Home from Church

The lilacs lift in generous bloom
   Their plumes of dear old-fashioned flowers;
Their fragrance fills the still old house
   Where left alone I count the hours.

High in the apple-trees the bees
   Are humming, busy in the sun,—
An idle robin cries for rain
   But once or twice and then is done.

The Sunday-morning quiet holds
   In heavy slumber all the street,
While from the church, just out of sight
   Behind the elms, comes slow and sweet

The organ's drone, the voices faint
   That sing the quaint long-meter hymn—
I somehow feel as if shut out
   From some mysterious temple, dim

And beautiful with blue and red
   And golden lights from windows high,
Where angels in the shadows stand
   And earth seems very near the sky.

The day-dream fades—and so I try
   Again to catch the tune that brings
No thought of temple nor of priest,
   But only of voice that sings.

A Caged Bird

High at the window in her cage
 The old canary flits and sings,
Nor sees across the curtain pass
 The shadow of a swallow's wings.

A poor deceit and copy, this,
 Of larger lives that mark their span,
Unreckoning of wider worlds
 Or gifts that Heaven keeps for man.

She gathers piteous bits and shreds,
 This solitary, mateless thing,
To patient build again the nest
 So rudely scattered spring by spring;

And sings her brief, unlistened songs,
 Her dreams of bird life wild and free,
Yet never beats her prison bars
 At sound of song from bush or tree.

But in my busiest hours I pause,
 Held by a sense of urgent speech,
Bewildered by that spark-like soul,
 Able my very soul to reach.

She will be heard; she chirps me loud,
 When I forget those gravest cares,
Her small provision to supply,
 Clear water or her seedsman's wares.

She begs me now for that chief joy
 The round great world is made to grow,—
Her wisp of greenness. Hear her chide,
 Because my answering thought is slow!

What can my life seem like to her?
A dull, unpunctual service mine;
Stupid before her eager call,
Her flitting steps, her insight fine.

To open wide thy prison door,
Poor friend, would give thee to thy foes;
And yet a plaintive note I hear,
As if to tell how slowly goes

The time of thy long prisoning.
Bird! does some promise keep thee sane?
Will there be better days for thee?
Will thy soul too know life again?

Ah, none of us have more than this:
If one true friend green leaves can reach
From out some fairer, wider place,
And understand our wistful speech!

EMMA LAZARUS
1849-1887

The New Ezekiel

What, can these dead bones live, whose sap is dried
By twenty scorching centuries of wrong?
Is this the House of Israel, whose pride
Is as a tale that's told, an ancient song?
Are these ignoble relics all that live
Of psalmist, priest, and prophet? Can the breath
Of very heaven bid these bones revive,
Open the graves and clothe the ribs of death?
Yea, Prophesy, the Lord hath said. Again
Say to the wind, Come forth and breathe afresh,
Even that they may live upon these slain,
And bone to bone shall leap, and flesh to flesh.
The Spirit is not dead, proclaim the word,
Where lay dead bones, a host of armed men stand!
I ope your graves, my people, saith the Lord,
And I shall place you living in your land.

Venus of the Louvre

Down the long hall she glistens like a star,
The foam-born mother of Love, transfixed to stone,
Yet none the less immortal, breathing on.
Time's brutal hand hath maimed but could not mar,
When first the enthralled enchantress from afar
Dazzled mine eyes, I saw not her alone,
Serenely poised on her world-worshipped throne,
As when she guided once her doze-drawn car,—
But at her feet a pale, death-stricken Jew,

Her life adorer, sobbed farewell to love.
Here *Heine* wept! Here still he weeps anew,
Nor ever shall his shadow lift or move,
While mourns one ardent heart, one poet-brain,
For vanished Hellas and Hebraic pain.

The South

Night, and beneath star-blazoned summer skies
   Behold the Spirit of the musky South,
A creole with still-burning, languid eyes,
   Voluptuous limbs and incense-breathing mouth:
     Swathed in spun gauze is she,
From fibres of her own anana tree.

Within these sumptuous woods she lies at ease.
   By rich night-breezes, dewy cool, caressed:
'Twixt cypresses and slim palmetto trees,
   Like to the golden oriole's hanging nest,
     Her airy hammock swings,
And through the dark her mocking-bird yet sings.

How beautiful she is! A tulip-wreath
   Twines round her shadowy, free-floating hair:
Young, weary, passionate, and sad as death,
   Dark visions haunt for her the vacant air,
     While movelessly she lies
With lithe, lax, folded hands and heavy eyes.

Full well knows she how wide and fair extend
   Her groves bright-flowered, her tangled everglades,
Majestic streams that indolently wend
    Through lush savanna or dense forest shades,
      Where the brown buzzard flies
To broad bayous 'neath hazy-golden skies.

Hers is the savage splendor of the swamp,
   With pomp of scarlet and of purple bloom,
Where blow warm, furtive breezes faint and damp,
    Strange insects whir, and stalking bitterns boom—
      Where from stale waters dead
Oft looms the great-jawed alligator's head.

Her wealth, her beauty, and the blight on these,—
   Of all she is aware: luxuriant woods,
Fresh, living, sunlit, in her dream she sees;
    And ever midst those verdant solitudes
      The soldier's wooden cross,
O'ergrown by creeping tendrils and rank moss.

Was hers a dream of empire? was it sin?
   And is it well that all was borne in vain?
She knows no more than one who slow doth win.
    After fierce fever, conscious life again,
      Too tired, too weak, too sad,
By the new light to be or stirred or glad.

From rich sea-islands fringing her green shore,
   From broad plantations where swart freemen bend
Bronzed backs in willing labor, from her store
    Of golden fruit, from stream, from town, ascend
      Life-currents of pure health:
Her aims shall be subserved with boundless wealth.

Yet now how listless and how still she lies,
    Like some half-savage, dusky Indian queen,
Rocked in her hammock 'neath her native skies,
    With the pathetic, passive, broken mien
        Of one who, sorely proved,
Great-souled, hath suffered much and much hath loved!

But look! along the wide-branched, dewy glade
    Glimmers the dawn: the light palmetto-trees
And cypresses reissue from the shade,
    And *she* hath wakened. Through clear air she sees
        The pledge, the brightening ray,
And leaps from dreams to hail the coming day.

JAMES WHITCOMB RILEY
1849-1916

Bereaved

Let me come in where you sit weeping,—ay,
    Let me, who have not any child to die,
Weep with you for the little one whose love
    I have known nothing of.

The little arms that slowly, slowly loosed
Their pressure round your neck; the hands you used
To kiss.—Such arms—such hands I never knew
    May I not weep with you?

Fain would I be of service—say something,
Between the tears, that would be comforting,—
But ah! so sadder than yourselves am I,
    Who have no child to die.

Katharine Lee Bates

1850-1929

America the Beautiful

O beautiful for spacious skies,
   For amber waves of grain,
For purple mountain majesties
   Above the fruited plain!
     America! America!
   God shed His grace on thee
And crown thy good with brotherhood
   From sea to shining sea!

O beautiful for pilgrim feet,
   Whose stern, impassioned stress
A thoroughfare for freedom beat
   Across the wilderness!
     America! America!
   God mend thine every flaw,
Confirm thy soul in self-control,
   Thy liberty in law!

O beautiful for heroes proved
   In liberating strife,
Who more than self their country loved,
   And mercy more than life!
     America! America!
   May God thy gold refine
Till all success be nobleness
   And every gain divine!

O beautiful for patriot dream
  That sees beyond the years
Thine alabaster cities gleam
  Undimmed by human tears!
    America! America!
  God shed His grace on thee
And crown thy good with brotherhood
  From sea to shining sea!

EUGENE FIELD

1850-1895

Wynken, Blynken, and Nod

Wynken, Blynken, and Nod one night
  Sailed off in a wooden shoe,—
Sailed on a river of crystal light
  Into a sea of dew.
"Where are you going, and what do you wish?"
  The old moon asked the three.
"We have come to fish for the herring-fish
  That live in this beautiful sea;
Nets of silver and gold have we,"
      Said Wynken,
      Blynken,
      And Nod.

The old moon laughed and sang a song,
  As they rocked in the wooden shoe;
And the wind that sped them all night long
  Ruffled the waves of dew;
The little stars were the herring-fish
  That lived in the beautiful sea.
"Now cast your nets wherever you wish,—
  Never afeard are we!"
So cried the stars to the fishermen three,
      Wynken,
      Blynken,
      And Nod.

All night long their nets they threw
  To the stars in the twinkling foam,—
Then down from the skies came the wooden shoe,
  Bringing the fishermen home:
'Twas all so pretty a sail, it seemed
  As if it could not be;
And some folk thought 'twas a dream they'd dreamed
  Of sailing that beautiful sea;
  But I shall name you the fishermen three:
      Wynken,
      Blynken,
      And Nod.

Wynken and Blynken are two little eyes,
  And Nod is a little head,
And the wooden shoe that sailed the skies
  Is a wee one's trundle-bed;
So shut your eyes while Mother sings
  Of wonderful sights that be,
And you shall see the beautiful things
  As you rock on the misty sea
  Where the old shoe rocked the fishermen three,—
      Wynken,
      Blynken,
      And Nod.

Little Boy Blue

The little toy dog is covered with dust,
　But sturdy and staunch he stands;
And the little toy soldier is red with rust,
　And his musket moulds in his hands.
Time was when the little toy dog was new,
　And the soldier was passing fair;
And that was the time when our Little Boy Blue
　Kissed them and put them there.

"Now, don't you go till I come," he said,
　"And don't you make any noise!"
So, toddling off to his trundle-bed,
　He dreamt of the pretty toys;
And, as he was dreaming, an angel song
　Awakened our Little Boy Blue—
Oh! the years are many, the years are long,
　But the little toy friends are true!

Ay, faithful to Little Boy Blue they stand,
　Each in the same old place,
Awaiting the touch of a little hand,
　The smile of a little face;
And they wonder, as waiting the long years through
　In the dust of that little chair,
What has become of our Little Boy Blue,
　Since he kissed them and put them there.

ELLA WHEELER WILCOX

1850-1919

Friendship After Love

After the fierce midsummer all ablaze
    Has burned itself to ashes, and expires
    In the intensity of its own fires,
There come the mellow, mild, St. Martin days
Crowned with the calm of peace, but sad with haze.
    So after Love has led us, till he tires
    Of his own throes, and torments, and desires,
Comes large-eyed friendship: with a restful gaze,
He beckons us to follow, and across
    Cool verdant vales we wander free from care.
    Is it a touch of frost lies in the air?
Why are we haunted with a sense of loss?
We do not wish the pain back, or the heat;
And yet, and yet, these days are incomplete.

The Year Outgrows the Spring

The year outgrows the spring it thought so sweet
    And clasps the summer with a new delight,
Yet wearied, leaves her languors and her heat
    When cool-browed autumn dawns upon his sight.

The tree outgrows the bud's suggestive grace
    And feels new pride in blossoms fully blown.
But even this to deeper joy gives place
    When bending boughs 'neath blushing burdens groan.

Life's rarest moments are derived from change,
  The heart outgrows old happiness, old grief,
And suns itself in feelings new and strange.
  The most enduring pleasure is but brief.

Our tastes, our needs, are never twice the same.
  Nothing contents us long, however dear.
The spirit in us, like the grosser frame,
  Outgrows the garments which it wore last year.

Change is the watchword of Progression. When
  We tire of well-worn ways, we seek for new.
This restless craving in the souls of men
  Spurs them to climb, and seek the mountain view.

So let who will erect an altar shrine
  To meek-browed Constancy, and sing her praise
Unto enlivening Change I shall build mine.
  Who lends new zest, and interest to my days.

EDWIN MARKHAM

1852-1940

The Man with the Hoe

God made man in His own image, in the image of God made He him.—GENESIS.

Written after seeing the Painting by Millet

Bowed by the weight of centuries he leans
Upon his hoe and gazes on the ground,
The emptiness of ages in his face,
And on his back the burden of the world.
Who made him dead to rapture and despair,
A thing that grieves not and that never hopes,
Stolid and stunned, a brother to the ox?
Who loosened and let down this brutal jaw?
Whose was the hand that slanted back this brow?
Whose breath blew out the light within this brain?

Is this the Thing the Lord God made and gave
To have dominion over sea and land;
To trace the stars and search the heavens for power;
To feel the passion of Eternity?
Is this the Dream He dreamed who shaped the suns
And pillared the blue firmament with light?
Down all the stretch of Hell to its last gulf
There is no shape more terrible than this—
More tongued with censure of the world's blind greed—
More filled with signs and portents for the soul—
More fraught with menace to the universe.

What gulfs between him and the seraphim!
Slave of the wheel of labor, what to him
Are Plato and the swing of Pleiades?

What the long reaches of the peaks of song,
The rift of dawn, the reddening of the rose?
Through this dread shape the suffering ages look;
Time's tragedy is in that aching stoop;
Through this dread shape humanity betrayed,
Plundered, profaned, and disinherited,
Cries protest to the Judges of the World,
A protest that is also prophecy.

O masters, lords, and rulers in all lands,
Is this the handiwork you give to God,
This monstrous thing distorted and soul-quenched?
How will you ever straighten up this shape;
Touch it again with immortality;
Give back the upward looking and the light;
Rebuild in it the music and the dream;
Make right the immemorial infamies,
Perfidious wrongs, immedicable woes?

O masters, lords, and rulers in all lands,
How will the Future reckon with this Man?
How answer his brute question in that hour
When whirlwinds of rebellion shake the world?
How will it be with kingdoms and with kings—
With those who shaped him to the thing he is—
When this dumb Terror shall reply to God,
After the silence of the centuries?

LIZETTE WOODWORTH REESE
1856-1935

A Puritan Lady

Wild Carthage held her, Rome,
  Sidon. She stared to tears
Tall, golden Helen, wearying
  Behind the Trojan spears.

Towered Antwerp knew her well;
  She wore her quiet gown
In some hushed house in Oxford grass,
  Or lane in Salem town.

Humble and high in one,
  Cool, certain, different,
She lasts; scarce saint, yet half a child,
  As hard, as innocent.

What grave, long afternoons,
  What caged airs round her blown,
Stripped her of humor, left her bare
  As cloud, or wayside stone?

Made her as clear a thing,
  In this slack world as plain
As a white flower on a grave,
  Or sleet sharp at a pane?

Wild Cherry

Why make your lodging here in this spent lane,
Where but an old man, with his sheep each day,
Twice through the forgotten grass goes by your way,
Half sees you there, and not once looks again?
For you are of the very ribs of spring,
And should have many lovers, who have none.
In silver cloaks, in hushed troops down the sun
Should they draw near, oh, strange and lovely thing!
Beauty has no set weather, no sure place;
Her careful pageantries are here as there,
With nothing lost. And soon, some lad may start—
A strayed Mayer in this unremembered space—
At your tall white, and know you very fair,
Let all else go to roof within your heart.

Hamlin Garland

1860-1940

A Tribute of Grasses
(*To W. W.*)

Serene, vast head, with silver cloud of hair
Lined on the purple dusk of death,
A stern medallion, velvet set—
Old Norseman, throned, not chained upon thy chair,
Thy grasp of hand, thy hearty breath
   Of welcome thrills me yet
   As when I faced thee there!

Loving my plain as thou thy sea,
Facing the East as thou the West,
I bring a handful of grass to thee—
The prairie grasses I know the best;
Type of the wealth and width of the plain,
Strong of the strength of the wind and sleet,
Fragrant with sunlight and cool with rain,
I bring it and lay it low at thy feet,
   Here by the eastern sea.

CHARLOTTE PERKINS GILMAN
1860-1935

A Common Inference

A night: mysterious, tender, quiet, deep;
Heavy with flowers; full of life asleep;
Thrilling with insect voices; thick with stars;
No cloud between the dewdrops and red Mars;
The small earth whirling softly on her way,
The moonbeams and the waterfalls at play;
A million million worlds that move in peace,
A million mighty laws that never cease;
And one small ant-heap, hidden by small weeds,
Rich with eggs, slaves, and store of millet seeds.
  They sleep beneath the sod
    And trust in God.

A day: all glorious, royal, blazing bright;
Heavy with flowers; full of life and light;
Great fields of corn and sunshine; courteous trees;
Snow-sainted mountains; earth-embracing seas;
Wide golden deserts; slender silver streams;
Clear rainbows where the tossing fountain gleams;
And everywhere, in happiness and peace,
A million forms of life that never cease;
And one small ant-heap, crushed by passing tread,
Hath scarce enough alive to mourn the dead!
  They shriek beneath the sod,
    "There is no God!"

HARRIET MONROE
1860-1936

Love Song

I love my life, but not too well
   To give it to thee like a flower,
So it may pleasure thee to dwell
   Deep in its perfume but an hour.
I love my life, but not too well.

I love my life, but not too well
   To sing it note by note away,
So to thy soul the song may tell
   The beauty of the desolate day.
I love my life, but not too well.

I love my life, but not too well
   To cast it like a cloak on thine,
Against the storms that sound and swell
   Between thy lonely heart and mine.
I love my life, but not too well.

EDITH WHARTON
1862-1937

The Mortal Lease

Yet for one rounded moment I will be
No more to you than what my lips may give,
And in the circle of your kisses live
As in some island of a storm-blown sea,
Where the cold surges of infinity
Upon the outward reefs unheeded grieve,
And the loud murmur of our blood shall weave
Primeval silences round you and me.

If in that moment we are all we are,
We live enough. Let this for all requite.
Do I not know, some wingèd things from far
Are borne along illimitable night
To dance their lives out in a single flight
Between the moonrise and the setting star?

STEPHEN CRANE

1871-1900

War Is Kind

Do not weep, maiden, for war is kind.
Because your lover threw wild hands toward the sky
And the affrighted steed ran on alone,
Do not weep.
War is kind.

> Hoarse, booming drums of the regiment,
> Little souls who thirst for fight,
> These men were born to drill and die.
> The unexplained glory flies above them,
> Great is the battle god, great, and his kingdom—
> A field where a thousand corpses lie.

Do not weep, babe, for war is kind.
Because your father tumbled in the yellow trenches,
Raged at his breast, gulped and died,
Do not weep.
War is kind.

> Swift blazing flag of the regiment,
> Eagle with crest of red and gold,
> These men were born to drill and die.
> Point for them the virtue of slaughter,
> Make plain to them the excellence of killing
> And a field where a thousand corpses lie.

Mother whose heart hung humble as a button
On the bright splendid shroud of your son,
Do not weep.
War is kind.

A God in Wrath

A god in wrath
Was beating a man;
He cuffed him loudly
With thunderous blows
That rang and rolled over the earth.
All people came running.
The man screamed and struggled,
And bit madly at the feet of the god.
The people cried,
"Ah, what a wicked man!"
And—
"Ah, what a redoubtable god!"

In the Desert

In the desert
I saw a creature, naked, bestial,
Who, squatting upon the ground,
Held his heart in his hands,
And ate of it.
I said, "Is it good, friend?"
"It is bitter—bitter," he answered,
"But I like it
Because it is bitter,
And because it is my heart."

A Man Said to the Universe

A man said to the universe:
"Sir, I exist!"
"However," replied the universe,
"The fact has not created in me
A sense of obligation."

Paul Laurence Dunbar

1872-1906

Ere Sleep Comes Down to Soothe the Weary Eyes

Ere sleep comes down to soothe the weary eyes,
Which all the day with ceaseless care have sought
The magic gold which from the seeker flies;
Ere dreams put on the gown and cap of thought,
And make the waking world a world of lies,—
Of lies most palpable, uncouth, forlorn,
That say life's full of aches and tears and sighs—
Oh, how with more than dreams the soul is torn,
Ere sleep comes down to soothe the weary eyes.

Ere sleep comes down to soothe the weary eyes,
How all the griefs and heartaches we have known
Come up like pois'nous vapors that arise
From some base witch's caldron, when the crone,
To work some potent spell, her magic plies.
The past which held its share of bitter pain,
Whose ghost we prayed that Time might exorcise,
Comes up, is lived and suffered o'er again,
Ere sleep comes down to soothe the weary eyes.

Ere sleep comes down to soothe the weary eyes,
What phantoms fill the dimly lighted room;
What ghostly shades in awe-creating guise
Are bodied forth within the teeming gloom.
What echoes faint of sad and soul-sick cries,
And pangs of vague inexplicable pain
That pay the spirit's ceaseless enterprise,
Come thronging through the chambers of the brain,
Ere sleep comes down to soothe the weary eyes.

Ere sleep comes down to soothe the weary eyes,
Where ranges forth the spirit far and free?
Through what strange realms and unfamiliar skies
Tends her far course to lands of mystery?
To lands unspeakable—beyond surmise,
Where shapes unknowable to being spring,
Till, faint of wing, the Fancy fails and dies
Much wearied with the spirit's journeying,
Ere sleep comes down to soothe the weary eyes.

Ere sleep comes down to soothe the weary eyes,
How questioneth the soul that other soul—
The inner sense which neither cheats nor lies,
But self exposes unto self, a scroll
Full writ with all life's acts unwise or wise,
In characters indelible and known;
So, trembling with the shock of sad surprise,
The soul doth view its awful self alone,
Ere sleep comes down to soothe the weary eyes.

When sleep comes down to seal the weary eyes,
The last dear sleep whose soft embrace is balm,
And whom sad sorrow teaches us to prize
For kissing all our passion into calm,
Ah, then, no more we heed the sad world's cries,
Or seek to probe th' eternal mystery,
Or fret our souls at long-withheld replies,
At glooms through which our visions cannot see,
When sleep comes down to seal the weary eyes.

The Haunted Oak

Pray why are you so bare, so bare,
   Oh, bough of the old oak-tree;
And why, when I go through the shade you throw,
   Runs a shudder over me?

My leaves were green as the best, I trow,
   And sap ran free in my veins,
But I saw in the moonlight dim and weird
   A guiltless victim's pains.

I bent me down to hear his sigh;
   I shook with his gurgling moan,
And I trembled sore when they rode away,
   And left him here alone.

They'd charged him with the old, old crime,
   And set him fast in jail:
Oh, why does the dog howl all night long,
   And why does the night wind wail?

He prayed his prayer and he swore his oath,
   And he raised his hand to the sky;
But the beat of hoofs smote on his ear,
   And the steady tread drew nigh.

Who is it rides by night, by night,
   Over the moonlit road?
And what is the spur that keeps the pace,
   What is the galling goad?

And now they beat at the prison door,
   "Ho, keeper, do not stay!
We are friends of him whom you hold within,
   And we fain would take him away

"From those who ride fast on our heels
    With mind to do him wrong;
They have no care for his innocence,
    And the rope they bear is long."

They have fooled the jailer with lying words,
    They have fooled the man with lies;
The bolts unbar, the locks are drawn,
    And the great door open flies.

Now they have taken him from the jail,
    And hard and fast they ride,
And the leader laughs low down in his throat,
    As they halt my trunk beside.

Oh, the judge, he wore a mask of black,
    And the doctor one of white,
And the minister, with his oldest son,
    Was curiously bedight.

Oh, foolish man, why weep you now?
    'Tis but a little space,
And the time will come when these shall dread
    The mem'ry of your face.

I feel the rope against my bark,
    And the weight of him in my grain,
I feel in the throe of his final woe
    The touch of my own last pain.

And never more shall leaves come forth
    On a bough that bears the ban;
I am burned with dread, I am dried and dead,
    From the curse of a guiltless man.

And ever the judge rides by, rides by,
　　And goes to hunt the deer,
And ever another rides his soul
　　In the guise of a mortal fear.

And ever the man he rides me hard,
　　And never a night stays he;
For I feel his curse as a haunted bough
　　On the trunk of a haunted tree.

WILLA CATHER

1873-1947

In Rose Time

Oh this is the joy of the rose;
That it blows
And goes.

Winter lasts a five-month,
    Spring-time stays but one;
Yellow blow the rye-fields
    When the rose is done.

Pines are clad at Yuletide
    When the birch is bare,
And the holly's greenest
    In the frosty air.

Sorrow keeps a stone house
    Builded grim and gray;
Pleasure hath a straw thatch
    Hung with lanterns gay.

On her petty savings
    Niggard Prudence thrives,
Passion, ere the moonset,
    Bleeds a thousand lives.

Virtue hath a warm heart—
    Folly's dead and drowned;
Friendship hath her own when
    Love is underground.

Poppies in Ludlow Castle

Through halls of vanished pleasure,
   And hold of vanished power,
And crypt of faith forgotten,
   I came to Ludlow tower.

A-top of arch and stairway,
   Of crypt and donjon cell,
Of council hall and chamber,
   Of wall and ditch and well,

High over grated arches
   Where clinging ivies run,
A thousand scarlet poppies
   Enticed the rising sun.

Upon the topmost turret,
   With death and damp below,—
Three hundred years of spoilage,—
   The crimson poppies grow.

This hall it was that bred him,
   These halls that knew him brave,
The gentlest English singer
   That fills an English grave.

How have they heart to blossom
   So cruel gay and red,
When beauty so hath perished.
   And valor so hath sped?

When knights so fair are rotten,
   And captains true asleep,
And singing lips are dust-stopped,
   Six English earth-feet deep?

When ages old remind me
    How much hath gone for naught,
What wretched ghost remaineth
    Of all that flesh hath wrought;

Of love and song and warring,
    Of adventure and play,
Of art and comely building,
    Of faith and form and fray.

I'll mind the flowers of pleasure,
    Of short-lived youth and sleep,
That drank the sunny weather
    Atop of Ludlow keep.

Robert Frost

1874-1963

Mending Wall

Something there is that doesn't love a wall,
That sends the frozen-ground-swell under it
And spills the upper boulders in the sun,
And makes gaps even two can pass abreast.
The work of hunters is another thing:
I have come after them and made repair
Where they have left not one stone on a stone,
But they would have the rabbit out of hiding,
To please the yelping dogs. The gaps I mean,
No one has seen them made or heard them made,
But at spring mending-time we find them there.
I let my neighbor know beyond the hill;
And on a day we meet to walk the line
And set the wall between us once again.
We keep the wall between us as we go.
To each the boulders that have fallen to each.
And some are loaves and some so nearly balls
We have to use a spell to make them balance:
"Stay where you are until our backs are turned!"
We wear our fingers rough with handling them.
Oh, just another kind of outdoor game,
One on a side. It comes to little more:
There where it is we do not need the wall:
He is all pine and I am apple orchard.
My apple trees will never get across
And eat the cones under his pines, I tell him.
He only says, "Good fences make good neighbors."
Spring is the mischief in me, and I wonder
If I could put a notion in his head:

"*Why* do they make good neighbors? Isn't it
Where there are cows? But here there are no cows.
Before I built a wall I'd ask to know
What I was walling in or walling out,
And to whom I was like to give offense.
Something there is that doesn't love a wall,
That wants it down." I could say, "Elves" to him,
But it's not elves exactly, and I'd rather
He said it for himself. I see him there,
Bringing a stone grasped firmly by the top
In each hand, like an old-stone savage armed.
He moves in darkness as it seems to me,
Not of woods only and the shade of trees.
He will not go behind his father's saying,
And he likes having thought of it so well
He says again, "Good fences make good neighbors."

Storm Fear

When the wind works against us in the dark,
And pelts with snow
The lower-chamber window on the east,
And whispers with a sort of stifled bark,
The beast,
"Come out! Come out!"—
It costs no inward struggle not to go,
Ah, no!
I count our strength,
Two and a child,
Those of us not asleep subdued to mark
How the cold creeps as the fire dies at length—
How drifts are piled,

Dooryard and road ungraded,
Till even the comforting barn grows far away,
And my heart owns a doubt
Whether 'tis in us to arise with day
And save ourselves unaided.

My November Guest

My Sorrow, when she's here with me,
   Thinks these dark days of autumn rain
Are beautiful as days can be;
She loves the bare, the withered tree;
   She walks the sodden pasture lane.

Her pleasure will not let me stay.
   She talks and I am fain to list:
She's glad the birds are gone away,
She's glad her simple worsted gray
   Is silver now with clinging mist.

The desolate, deserted trees,
   The faded earth, the heavy sky,
The beauties she so truly sees,
She thinks I have no eye for these,
   And vexes me for reason why.

Not yesterday I learned to know
   The love of bare November days
Before the coming of the snow,
But it were vain to tell her so,
   And they are better for her praise.

The Death of the Hired Man

Mary sat musing on the lamp-flame at the table,
Waiting for Warren. When she heard his step,
She ran on tiptoe down the darkened passage
To meet him in the doorway with the news
And put him on his guard. "Silas is back."
She pushed him outward with her through the door
And shut it after her. "Be kind," she said.
She took the market things from Warren's arms
And set them on the porch, then drew him down
To sit beside her on the wooden steps.

"When was I ever anything but kind to him?
But I'll not have the fellow back," he said.
"I told him so last haying, didn't I?
If he left then, I said, that ended it.
What good is he? Who else will harbor him
At his age for the little he can do?
What help he is there's no depending on.
Off he goes always when I need him most.
He thinks he ought to earn a little pay,
Enough at least to buy tobacco with,
So he won't have to beg and be beholden.
'All right,' I say, 'I can't afford to pay
Any fixed wages, though I wish I could.'
'Someone else can.' 'Then someone else will have to.'
I shouldn't mind his bettering himself
If that was what it was. You can be certain,
When he begins like that, there's someone at him
Trying to coax him off with pocket money—
In haying time, when any help is scarce.
In winter he comes back to us. I'm done."

"Sh! not so loud: he'll hear you," Mary said.

"I want him to: he'll have to soon or late."

"He's worn out. He's asleep beside the stove.
When I came up from Rowe's I found him here,
Huddled against the barn door fast asleep,
A miserable sight, and frightening, too—
You needn't smile—I didn't recognize him—
I wasn't looking for him—and he's changed.
Wait till you see."

                    "Where did you say he'd been?"

"He didn't say. I dragged him to the house.
And gave him tea and tried to make him smoke.
I tried to make him talk about his travels.
Nothing would do: he just kept nodding off."

"What did he say? Did he say anything?"

"But little."

                    "Anything? Mary, confess
He said he'd come to ditch the meadow for me."

"Warren!"

          "But did he? I just want to know."

"Of course he did. What would you have him say?
Surely you wouldn't grudge the poor old man
Some humble way to save his self-respect.
He added, if you really care to know,
He meant to clear the upper pasture, too.
That sounds like something you have heard before?
Warren, I wish you could have heard the way
He jumbled everything. I stopped to look

Two or three times—he made me feel so queer—
To see if he was talking in his sleep.
He ran on Harold Wilson—you remember—
The boy you had in haying four years since.
He's finished school, and teaching in his college.
Silas declares you'll have to get him back.
He says they two will make a team for work:
Between them they will lay this farm as smooth!
The way he mixed that in with other things.
He thinks young Wilson a likely lad, though daft
On education—you know how they fought
All through July under the blazing sun,
Silas up on the cart to build the load,
Harold along beside to pitch it on."

"Yes, I took care to keep well out of earshot."

"Well, those days trouble Silas like a dream.
You wouldn't think they would. How some things linger!
Harold's young college-boy's assurance piqued him.
After so many years he still keeps finding
Good arguments he sees he might have used.
I sympathize. I know just how it feels
To think of the right thing to say too late.
Harold's associated in his mind with Latin.
He asked me what I thought of Harold's saying
He studied Latin, like the violin,
Because he liked it—that an argument!
He said he couldn't make the boy believe
He could find water with a hazel prong—
Which showed how much good school had ever done
    him.

He wanted to go over that. But most of all
He thinks if he could have another chance
To teach him how to build a load of hay—"

"I know, that's Silas' one accomplishment.
He bundles every forkful in its place,
And tags and numbers it for future reference,
So he can find and easily dislodge it
In the unloading, Silas does that well.
He takes it out in bunches like big birds' nests.
You never see him standing on the hay
He's trying to lift, straining to lift himself."

"He thinks if he could teach him that, he'd be
Some good perhaps to someone in the world.
He hates to see a boy the fool of books.
Poor Silas, so concerned for other folk,
And nothing to look backward to with pride,
And nothing to look forward to with hope,
So now and never any different."

Part of a moon was falling down the west,
Dragging the whole sky with it to the hills.
Its light poured softly in her lap. She saw it
And spread her apron to it. She put out her hand
Among the harplike morning-glory strings,
Taut with the dew from garden bed to eaves,
As if she played unheard some tenderness
That wrought on him beside her in the night.
"Warren," she said, "he has come home to die:
You needn't be afraid he'll leave you this time."

"Home," he mocked gently.

                "Yes, what else but home?
It all depends on what you mean by home.
Of course he's nothing to us, any more
Than was the hound that came a stranger to us
Out of the woods, worn out upon the trail."

"Home is the place where, when you have to go there,
They have to take you in."

               "I should have called it
Something you somehow haven't to deserve."

Warren leaned out and took a step or two,
Picked up a little stick, and brought it back
And broke it in his hand and tossed it by.
"Silas has better claim on us you think
Than on his brother? Thirteen little miles
As the road winds would bring him to his door.
Silas has walked that far no doubt today.
Why doesn't he go there? His brother's rich,
A somebody—director in the bank."

"He never told us that."

               "We know it, though."

"I think his brother ought to help, of course.
I'll see to that if there is need. He ought of right
To take him in, and might be willing to—
He may be better than appearances.
But have some pity on Silas. Do you think
If he had any pride in claiming kin
Or anything he looked for from his brother,
He'd keep so still about him all this time?"

"I wonder what's between them."

                                            "I can tell you.
Silas is what he is—we wouldn't mind him—
But just the kind that kinsfolk can't abide.
He never did a thing so very bad.
He don't know why he isn't quite as good
As anybody. Worthless though he is,
He won't be made ashamed to please his brother."

"*I* can't think Si ever hurt anyone."

"No, but he hurt my heart the way he lay
And rolled his old head on that sharp-edged chair-back.
He wouldn't let me put him on the lounge.
You must go in and see what you can do.
I made the bed up for him there tonight.
You'll be surprised at him—how much he's broken.
His working days are done; I'm sure of it."

"I'd not be in a hurry to say that."

"I haven't been. Go, look, see for yourself.
But, Warren, please remember how it is:
He's come to help you ditch the meadow.
He has a plan. You mustn't laugh at him.
He may not speak of it, and then he may.
I'll sit and see if that small sailing cloud
Will hit or miss the moon."

                              It hit the moon.
Then there were three there, making a dim row,
The moon, the little silver cloud, and she.

Warren returned—too soon, it seemed to her—
Slipped to her side, caught up her hand and waited.

"Warren?" she questioned.

                        "Dead," was all he answered.

Home Burial

He saw her from the bottom of the stairs
Before she saw him. She was starting down,
Looking back over her shoulder at some fear.
She took a doubtful step and then undid it
To raise herself and look again. He spoke
Advancing toward her: "What is it you see
From up there always?—for I want to know."
She turned and sank upon her skirts at that,
And her face changed from terrified to dull.
He said to gain time: "What is it you see?"
Mounting until she cowered under him.
"I will find out now—you must tell me, dear."
She, in her place, refused him any help,
With the least stiffening of her neck and silence.
She let him look, sure that he wouldn't see,
Blind creature; and awhile he didn't see.
But at last he murmured, "Oh," and again, "Oh."

"What is it—what?" she said.

                                    "Just that I see."

"You don't," she challenged. "Tell me what it is."

"The wonder is I didn't see at once.
I never noticed it from here before.
I must be wonted to it—that's the reason.
The little graveyard where my people are!
So small the window frames the whole of it.
Not so much larger than a bedroom, is it?
There are three stones of slate and one of marble,
Broad-shouldered little slabs there in the sunlight
On the sidehill. We haven't to mind *those*.

But I understand: it is not the stones,
But the child's mound—"

                     "Don't, don't, don't,

   don't," she cried.

She withdrew, shrinking from beneath his arm
That rested on the banister, and slid downstairs;
And turned on him with such a daunting look,
He said twice over before he knew himself:
"Can't a man speak of his own child he's lost?"

"Not you!—Oh, where's my hat? Oh, I don't need it!
I must get out of here. I must get air.—
I don't know rightly whether any man can."
"Amy! Don't go to someone else this time.
Listen to me. I won't come down the stairs."
He sat and fixed his chin between his fists.
"There's something I should like to ask you, dear."

"You don't know how to ask it."

                     "Help me, then."

Her fingers moved the latch for all reply.

"My words are nearly always an offense.
I don't know how to speak of anything
So as to please you. But I might be taught,
I should suppose. I can't say I see how.
A man must partly give up being a man
With womenfolk. We could have some arrangement
By which I'd bind myself to keep hands off
Anything special you're a-mind to name.
Though I don't like such things 'twixt those that love.
Two that don't love can't live together without them.

But two that do can't live together with them."
She moved the latch a little. "Don't—don't go.
Don't carry it to someone else this time.
Tell me about it if it's something human.
Let me into your grief. I'm not so much
Unlike other folks as your standing there
Apart would make me out. Give me my chance.
I do think, though you overdo it a little.
What was it brought you up to think it the thing
To take your mother-loss of a first child
So inconsolably—in the face of love.
You'd think his memory might be satisfied—"

"There you go sneering now!"

                              "I'm not, I'm not!
You make me angry. I'll come down to you.
God, what a woman! And it's come to this,
A man can't speak of his own child that's dead."

"You can't because you don't know how to speak.
If you had any feelings, you that dug
With your own hand—how could you?—his little grave;
I saw you from that very window there,
Making the gravel leap and leap in air,
Leap up, like that, like that, and land so lightly
And roll back down the mound beside the hole.

I thought, Who is that man? I didn't know you.
And I crept down the stairs and up the stairs
To look again, and still your spade kept lifting.
Then you came in. I heard your rumbling voice
Out in the kitchen, and I don't know why,
But I went near to see with my own eyes.
You could sit there with the stains on your shoes

Of the fresh earth from your own baby's grave
And talk about your everyday concerns.
You had stood the spade up against the wall
Outside there in the entry, for I saw it."

"I shall laugh the worst laugh I ever laughed.
I'm cursed. God, if I don't believe I'm cursed."

"I can repeat the very words you were saying:
'Three foggy mornings and one rainy day
Will rot the best birch fence a man can build.'
Think of it, talk like that at such a time!
What had how long it takes a birch to rot
To do with what was in the darkened parlor?
You *couldn't* care! The nearest friends can go
With anyone to death, comes so far short
They might as well not try to go at all.
No, from the time when one is sick to death,
One is alone, and he dies more alone.
Friends make pretense of following to the grave,
But before one is in it, their minds are turned
And making the best of their way back to life
And living people, and things they understand.
But the world's evil. I won't have grief so
If I can change it. Oh, I won't, I won't!"

"There, you have said it all and you feel better.
You won't go now. You're crying. Close the door.
The heart's gone out of it: why keep it up?
Amy! There's someone coming down the road!"

"*You*—oh, you think the talk is all. I must go—
Somewhere out of this house. How can I make you—"

"If—you—do!" She was opening the door wider.
"Where do you mean to go? First tell me that.
I'll follow and bring you back by force. I *will!*—"

After Apple-Picking

My long two-pointed ladder's sticking through a tree
Toward heaven still,
And there's a barrel that I didn't fill
Beside it, and there may be two or three
Apples I didn't pick upon some bough.
But I am done with apple-picking now.
Essence of winter sleep is on the night,
The scent of apples: I am drowsing off.
I cannot rub the strangeness from my sight
I got from looking through a pane of glass
I skimmed this morning from the drinking trough
And held against the world of hoary grass.
It melted, and I let it fall and break.
But I was well
Upon my way to sleep before it fell,
And I could tell
What form my dreaming was about to take.
Magnified apples appear and disappear,
Stem end and blossom end,
And every fleck of russet showing clear.
My instep arch not only keeps the ache,
It keeps the pressure of a ladder-round.
I feel the ladder sway as the boughs bend,
And I keep hearing from the cellar bin
The rumbling sound
Of load on load of apples coming in.

For I have had too much
Of apple-picking: I am overtired
Of the great harvest I myself desired.
There were ten thousand thousand fruit to touch,
Cherish in hand, lift down, and not let fall.
For all
That struck the earth,
No matter if not bruised or spiked with stubble,
Went surely to the cider-apple heap
As of no worth.
One can see what will trouble
This sleep of mine, whatever sleep it is.
Were he not gone,
The woodchuck could say whether it's like his
Long sleep, as I describe its coming on,
Or just some human sleep.

The Wood-Pile

Out walking in the frozen swamp one gray day,
I paused and said, "I will turn back from here.
No, I will go on farther—and we shall see."
The hard snow held me, save where now and then
One foot went through. The view was all in lines
Straight up and down of tall slim trees
Too much alike to mark or name a place by
So as to say for certain I was here
Or somewhere else: I was just far from home.
A small bird flew before me. He was careful
To put a tree between us when he lighted,
And say no word to tell me who he was
Who was so foolish as to think what *he* thought.

He thought that I was after him for a feather—
The white one in his tail; like one who takes
Everything said as personal to himself.
One flight out sideways would have undeceived him.
And then there was a pile of wood for which
I forgot him and let his little fear
Carry him off the way I might have gone,
Without so much as wishing him good-night.
He went behind it to make his last stand.
It was a cord of maple, cut and split
And piled—and measured, four by four by eight.
And not another like it could I see.
No runner tracks in this year's snow looped near it.
And it was older sure than this year's cutting,
Or even last year's or the year's before.
The wood was gray and the bark warping off it
And the pile somewhat sunken. Clematis
Had wound strings round and round it like a bundle.
What held it, though, on one side was a tree
Still growing, and on one a stake and prop,
These latter about to fall. I thought that only
Someone who lived in turning to fresh tasks
Could so forget his handiwork on which
He spent himself, the labor of his ax,
And leave it there far from a useful fireplace
To warm the frozen swamp as best it could
With the slow smokeless burning of decay.

The Road Not Taken

Two roads diverged in a yellow wood,
And sorry I could not travel both
And be one traveler, long I stood
And looked down one as far as I could
To where it bent in the undergrowth;

Then took the other, as just as fair,
And having perhaps the better claim,
Because it was grassy and wanted wear;
Though as for that, the passing there
Had worn them really about the same,

And both that morning equally lay
In leaves no step had trodden black.
Oh, I kept the first for another day!
Yet knowing how way leads on to way,
I doubted if I should ever come back.

I shall be telling this with a sigh
Somewhere ages and ages hence:
Two roads diverged in a wood, and I—
I took the one less traveled by,
And that has made all the difference.

The Oven Bird

There is a singer everyone has heard,
Loud, a mid-summer and a mid-wood bird,
Who makes the solid tree trunks sound again.
He says that leaves are old and that for flowers
Mid-summer is to spring as one to ten.
He says the early petal-fall is past,

When pear and cherry bloom went down in showers
On sunny days a moment overcast;
And comes that other fall we name the fall.
He says the highway dust is over all.
The bird would cease and be as other birds
But that he knows in singing not to sing.
The question that he frames in all but words
Is what to make of a diminished thing.

"Out, Out—"

The buzz saw snarled and rattled in the yard
And made dust and dropped stove-length sticks of wood,
Sweet-scented stuff when the breeze drew across it.
And from there those that lifted eyes could count
Five mountain ranges one behind the other
Under the sunset far into Vermont.
And the saw snarled and rattled, snarled and rattled,
As it ran light, or had to bear a load.
And nothing happened: day was all but done.
Call it a day, I wish they might have said
To please the boy by giving him the half hour
That a boy counts so much when saved from work.
His sister stood beside them in her apron
To tell them "Supper," At the word, the saw,
As if to prove saws knew what supper meant,
Leaped out at the boy's hand, or seemed to leap—
He must have given the hand. However it was,
Neither refused the meeting. But the hand!
The boy's first outcry was a rueful laugh,
As he swung toward them holding up the hand,
Half in appeal, but half as if to keep

The life from spilling. Then the boy saw all—
Since he was old enough to know, big boy
Doing a man's work, though a child at heart—
He saw all spoiled. "Don't let him cut my hand off—
The doctor, when he comes. Don't let him, sister!"
So. But the hand was gone already.
The doctor put him in the dark of ether.
He lay and puffed his lips out with his breath.
And then—the watcher at his pulse took fright.
No one believed. They listened at his heart.
Little—less—nothing!—and that ended it.
No more to build on there. And they, since they
Were not the one dead, turned to their affairs.

Birches

When I see birches bend to left and right
Across the lines of straighter darker trees,
I like to think some boy's been swinging them.
But swinging doesn't bend them down to stay
As ice storms do. Often you must have seen them
Loaded with ice a sunny winter morning
After a rain. They click upon themselves
As the breeze rises, and turn many colored
As the stir cracks and crazes their enamel.
Soon the sun's warmth makes them shed crystal shells
Shattering and avalanching on the snow crust—
Such heaps of broken glass to sweep away
You'd think the inner dome of heaven had fallen.
They are dragged to the withered bracken by the load,
And they seem not to break; though once they are
    bowed

So low for long, they never right themselves:
You may see their trunks arching in the woods
Years afterwards, trailing their leaves on the ground
Like girls on hands and knees that throw their hair
Before them over their heads to dry in the sun.
But I was going to say when Truth broke in
With all her matter of fact about the ice storm,
I should prefer to have some boy bend them
As he went out and in to fetch the cows—
Some boy too far from town to learn baseball,
Whose only play was what he found himself,
Summer or winter, and could play alone.
One by one he subdued his father's trees
By riding them down over and over again
Until he took the stiffness out of them,
And not one but hung limp, not one was left
For him to conquer. He learned all there was
To learn about not launching out too soon
And so not carrying the tree away
Clear to the ground. He always kept his poise
To the top branches, climbing carefully
With the same pains you use to fill a cup
Up to the brim, and even above the brim.
Then he flung outward, feet first, with a swish,
Kicking his way down through the air to the ground.
So was I once myself a swinger of birches.
And so I dream of going back to be.
It's when I'm weary of considerations,
And life is too much like a pathless wood
Where your face burns and tickles with the cobwebs
Broken across it, and one eye is weeping
From a twig's having lashed across it open.
I'd like to get away from earth awhile

And then come back to it and begin over.
May no fate willfully misunderstand me
And half grant what I wish and snatch me away
Not to return. Earth's the right place for love:
I don't know where it's likely to go better.
I'd like to go by climbing a birch tree,
And climb black branches up a snow-white trunk
Toward heaven, till the tree could bear no more,
But dipped its top and set me down again.
That would be good both going and coming back.
One could do worse than be a swinger of birches.

Amy Lowell

1874-1925

Meeting-House Hill

I must be mad, or very tired,
When the curve of a blue bay beyond a railroad track
Is shrill and sweet to me like the sudden springing of
a tune,
And the sight of a white church above thin trees in a
city square
Amazes my eyes as though it were the Parthenon.
Clear, reticent, superbly final,
With the pillars of its portico refined to a cautious
elegance,
It dominates the weak trees,
And the shot of its spire
Is cool, and candid,
Rising into an unresisting sky,
Strange meeting-house
Pausing a moment upon a squalid hill-top.
I watch the spire sweeping the sky,
I am dizzy with the movement of the sky,
I might be watching a mast
With its royals set full
Straining before a two-reef breeze.
I might be sighting a tea-clipper,
Tacking into the blue bay,
Just back from Canton
With her hold full of green and blue porcelain,
And a Chinese coolie leaning over the rail
Gazing at the white spire
With dull, sea-spent eyes.

The Taxi

When I go away from you
The world bears dead
Like a slackened drum.
I call out for you against the jutted stars
And shout into the ridges of the wind.
Streets coming fast,
One after the other,
Wedge you away from me,
And the lamps of the city prick my eyes
So that I can no longer see your face.
Why should I leave you,
To wound myself upon the sharp edges of the night?

Chinoiseries

Reflections

When I looked into your eyes,
I saw a garden
With peonies, and tinkling pagodas,
And round-arched bridges
Over still lakes.
A woman sat beside the water
In a rain-blue, silken garment.
She reached through the water
To pluck the crimson peonies
Beneath the surface,
But as she grasped the stems,

They jarred and broke into white-green ripples;
And as she drew out her hand,
The water-drops dripping from it
Stained her rain-blue dress like tears.

Falling Snow

The snow whispers about me,
And my wooden clogs
Leave holes behind me in the snow.
But no one will pass this way
Seeking my footsteps,
And when the temple bell rings again
They will be covered and gone.

Hoar-Frost

In the cloud-gray mornings
I heard the herons flying;
And when I came into my garden,
My silken outer-garment
Trailed over withered leaves.
A dried leaf crumbles at a touch,
But I have seen many Autumns
With herons blowing like smoke
Across the sky.

Apology

Be not angry with me that I bear
   Your colors everywhere,
All through each crowded street,
   And meet
The wonder-light in every eye,
As I go by.

Each plodding wayfarer looks up to gaze
Blinded by rainbow-haze,
The stuff of happiness,
   No less,
Which wraps me in its glad-hued folds
Of peacock golds.

Before my feet the dusty, rough-paved way
Flushes beneath its gray.
My steps fall ringed with light,
   So bright
It seems a myriad suns are strown
About the town.

You blazen me with jewelled insignia.
A flaming nebula
Rims in my life. And yet
You set
The word upon me, unconfessed,
To go unguessed.

TRUMBULL STICKNEY
1874-1904

In the Past

There lies a somnolent lake
Under a noiseless sky,
Where never the mornings break
Nor the evenings die.

Mad flakes of colour
Whirl on its even face
Iridescent and streaked with pallour;
And, warding the silent place,

The rocks rise sheer and gray
From the sedgeless brink to the sky
Dull-lit with the light of pale half-day
Thro' a void space and dry.

And the hours lag dead in the air
With a sense of coming eternity
To the heart of the lonely boatman there:
That boatman am I,

I, in my lonely boat,
A waif on the somnolent lake,
Watching the colours creep and float
With the sinuous track of a snake.

Now I lean o'er the side
And lazy shades in the water see,
Lapped in the sweep of a sluggish tide
Crawled in from the living sea;

And next I fix mine eyes,
So long that the heart declines,
On the changeless face of the open skies
Where no star shines;

And now to the rocks I turn,
To the rocks, around
That lie like walls of a circling urn
Wherein lie bound

The waters that feel my powerless strength
And meet my homeless oar
Labouring over their ashen length
Never to find a shore.

But the gleam still skims
At times on the somnolent lake,
And a light there is that swims
With the whirl of a snake;

And tho' dead be the hours i' the air,
And dayless the sky,
The heart is alive of the boatman there:
That boatman am I.

Quiet After the Rain of Morning

Quiet after the rain of morning
Midday covers the dampened trees;
Sweet and fresh in the languid breeze
Still returning
Birds are twittering at ease.

And to me in the far and foreign
Land as further I go and come,
Sweetly over the wearisome
Endless barren
Flutter whisperings of home.

There between the two hillocks lightens
Straight and little a bluish bar:
I feel the strain of the mariner
Grows and tightens
After home and after her.

Pity

An old light smoulders in her eye.
There she looks up. They grow and glow
Like mad laughs of a rhapsody
That flickers out in woe.

An old charm slips into her sighs,
An old grace sings about her hand.
She bends: it's musically wise.
I cannot understand.

Her voice is strident; but a spell
Of fluted whisper silkens in—
The lost heart in a moss-grown bell,
Faded—but sweet—but thin.

She bows like waves—waves near the shore.
Her hair is in a vulgar knot—
Lovely, dark hair, whose curves deplore
Something she's well forgot.

She must have known the sun, the moon,
On heaven's warm throat star-jewels strung—
It's late. The gas-lights flicker on.
Young, only in years, but young!

One might remind her, say the street
Is dark and vile now day is done.
But would she care, she fear to meet—
But there she goes—is gone.

Requiescam

Come to the window! You're the painter used
To shadow-in pools of light far out to sea,
Or fix it where the solitary wave
Rears with a shimmering scoop before the shore,—
A glorious wave! But now look out awhile
And love my view, from our suburban height
The squalid champaign zigzagged by the Seine.

I'm old, most of my labour done. My chisel
One of these days among the pellets of dry clay
Will lie and rust. I have immensely worked,
And hitherto seen nothing but the Form

Staring upon my eyeballs. Years and years.
Whether alone along the shining streets
O' the city or in companionship, I've looked
So long and seen away so fixedly
That space scrolled up, I seeing none the less:
Except some shape, some woman lightning-blenched,
Pinned to the ground, lay dreadful in my road.
O Labour, everlasting vanity,
That fills her cracking pitcher and falls down
Face to the earth, the water in her hair!

Into a bole of clay all my life long
I've stared my visions in, and, thumbing, seen
Materialize obscurely to a line
The long desire of Nature turning home.
So strains itself out of the sea a shape
With loads of weedy tide up to the land,
Straining to touch and taste, to lose and die,
Straining fore'er miserably unsatisfied.
Between the toad and lyre-bird, 'twixt the snail
And greyhound all is struggle: the which is vain.
For by our bases we're firm sunken-down
In the element: and whenever a little while
Yearning Illusion flutters up the sky,
She presently swings to the gasping pitch,
To fall bolt-like.

I say, all my life long close to I've stared
Into the clay, have with my chisel rasped
The marble off and stroked the lovely limbs,
The breasts of women and the lips of boys
In stone. Again, into the mould I've poured
The wretched desolation of my dreams
And bruisèd here and there the bronze. All this

I had done my life long, and not so much
As lifted up my eyes.
               But now at last
I pleasurably look to either side.
For I would paint some landscapes ere I die,
One or two landscapes of the view you see,
The squalid plain meandered by the Seine.
There, when there's moon, thro' fumes of gray and black
The silver river curls away; beyond
It's night and vapid darkness infinite.
And sitting at this window, I suppose
A pallet on my thumb, and brushes and
The colours gently mixing with their oil:—
Leaving my marbles in imagination
For final solace in a softer art.
You, painter, have enjoyed with all your self;
You've little looked into the dark. But I
Forged in the night. It's resting-time, I'm old.
Landscape will ease me somewhat toward the end.

ADELAIDE CRAPSEY
1878-1914

Dirge

Never the nightingale,
  Oh, my dear,
Never again the lark
  Thou wilt hear;
Though dusk and the morning still
Tap at thy window-sill,
Though ever love call and call
Thou wilt not hear at all,
  My dear, my dear.

Vendor's Song

My songs to sell, good sir!
  I pray you buy.
Here's one will win a lady's tears,
  Here's one will make her gay.
Here's one will charm your true love true
  Forever and a day;
Good sir, I pray you buy!

Oh, no, he will not buy.

My songs to sell, sweet maid!
  I pray you buy.
This one will teach you Lilich's lore,
  And this what Helen knew,
And this will keep your gold hair gold,
  And this your blue eyes blue;
Sweet maid, I pray you buy!

Oh, no she will not buy.

If I'd as much money as I could tell,
I never would cry my songs to sell,
I never would cry my songs to sell.

Amaze

I know
Not these my hands
And yet I think there was
A woman like me once had hands
Like these.

November Night

Listen . . .
With faint dry sound,
Like steps of passing ghosts,
The leaves, frost-crisp'd, break from the trees
And fall.

VACHEL LINDSAY
1879-1931

Abraham Lincoln Walks at Midnight

It is portentous, and a thing of state
That here at midnight, in our little town
A mourning figure walks, and will not rest,
Near the old court-house pacing up and down.

Or by his homestead, or in shadowed yards
He lingers where his children used to play,
Or through the market, on the well-worn stones
He stalks until the dawn-stars burn away.

A bronzed, lank man! His suit of ancient black,
A famous high-top hat and plain worn shawl
Make him the quaint great figure that men love,
The prairie lawyer, master of us all.

He cannot sleep upon his hillside now.
He is among us:—as in times before!
And we who toss and lie awake for long
Breathe deep, and start, to see him pass the door.

His head is bowed. He thinks on men and kins.
Yea, when the sick world cries, how can he sleep?
Too many peasants fight, they know not why,
Too many homesteads in black terror weep.

The sins of all the war-lords burn his heart.
He sees the dreadnaughts scouring every main.
He carries on his shawl-wrapped shoulders now
The bitterness, the folly and the pain.

He cannot rest until a spirit-dawn
Shall come:—the shining hope of Europe free:
The league of sober folk, the Workers' Earth,
Bringing long peace to Cornland, Alp and Sea.

It breaks his heart that kings must murder still,
That all his hours of travail here for men
Seem yet in vain. And who will bring white peace
That he may sleep upon his hill again?

SARA TEASDALE
1884-1933

Since There is No Escape

Since there is no escape, since at the end
   My body will be utterly destroyed,
This hand I love as I have loved a friend,
   This body I tended, wept with and enjoyed;
Since there is no escape even for me
   Who love life with a love too sharp to bear:
The scent of orchards in the rain, the sea
   And hours alone too still and sure for prayer—
Since darkness waits for me, then all the more
Let me go down as waves sweep to the shore
   In pride, and let me sing with my last breath;
In these few hours of light I lift my head;
Life is my lover—I shall leave the dead
   If there is any way to baffle death.

Open Windows

Out of the window a sea of green trees
   Lift their soft boughs like the arms of a dancer;
They beckon and call me, "Come out in the sun!"
   But I cannot answer.

I am alone with Weakness and Pain,
   Sick abed and June is going,
I cannot keep her, she hurries by
   With the silver-green of her garments blowing.

Men and women pass in the street
　Glad of the shining sapphire weather;
But we know more of it than they,
　Pain and I together.

They are the runners in the sun,
　Breathless and blinded by the race,
But we are watchers in the shade
　Who speak with Wonder face to face.

Barter

Life has loveliness to sell—
All beautiful and splendid things,
Blue waves whitened on a cliff,
Climbing fire that sways and sings,
And children's faces looking up
Holding wonder like a cup.

Life has loveliness to sell—
Music like a curve of gold,
Scent of pine trees in the rain,
Eyes that love you, arms that hold,
And for your spirit's still delight,
Holy thoughts that star the night.

Spend all you have for loveliness,
Buy it and never count for cost;
For one white singing hour of peace
Count many a year of strife well lost,
And for a breath of ecstasy
Give all you have been or could be.

Over the Roofs

I said, "I have shut my heart,
  As one shuts an open door,
That Love may starve therein
  And trouble me no more."

But over the roofs there came
  The wet new wind of May,
And a tune blew up from the curb
  Where the street-pianos play.

My room was white with the sun
  And Love cried out in me,
"I am strong, I will break your heart
  Unless you set me free."

I Would Live in Your Love

I would live in your love as the sea-grasses live in the sea,
Borne up by each wave as it passes, drawn down by each wave that
    recedes;
I would empty my soul of the dreams that have gathered in me,
I would beat with your heart as it beats, I would follow your soul as
    it leads.

The Flight

Look back with longing eyes and know that I will follow,
Lift me up in your love as a light wing lifts a swallow,
Let our flight be far in sun or blowing rain—
But what if I heard my first love calling me again?

Hold me on your heart as the brave sea holds the foam,
Take me far away to the hills that hide your home:
Peace shall thatch the roof and love shall latch the door—
But what if I heard my first love calling me once more?

Those Who Love

Those who love the most,
Do not talk of their love,
Francesca, Guinevere,
Deirdre, Iseult, Heloise,
In the fragrant gardens of heaven
Are silent, or speak if at all
Of fragile inconsequent things.

And a woman I used to know
Who loved one man from her youth,
Against the strength of the fates
Fighting in somber pride
Never spoke of this thing,
But hearing his name by chance,
A light would pass over her face.

The Gift

What can I give you, my lord, my lover,
You who have given the world to me,
Showed me the light and the joy that cover
The wild sweet earth and the restless sea?

All that I have are gifts of your giving—
If I gave them again, you would find them old,
And your soul would weary of always living
Before the mirror my life would hold.

What shall I give you, my lord, my lover?
The gift that breaks the heart in me:
I bid you awake at dawn and discover
I have gone my way and left you free.

WILLIAM ROSE BENÉT
1886-1950

The Woodcutter's Wife

Times she'll sit quiet by the hearth, and times
She'll ripple with a fit of twinkling rhymes
And rise and pirouette and flirt her hand,
Strut jackdaw-like, or stamp a curt command
Or, from behind my chair, suddenly blind me;
Then, when I turn, be vanished from behind me.

Times she'll be docile as the gentlest thing
That ever blinked in fur or folded wing,
And then, like lightning in the dead of night,
Fill with wild, crackling, intermitting light
My mind and soul and senses,—and next be
Aloof, askance as a dryad in a tree.

Then she'll be gone for days; when next I turn,
There, coaxing yellow butter from the churn,
Rubbing to silver every pan of tin,
Or conjuring color from the rooms within
Through innocent flowers, she'll hum about the house
Bright-eyed and secret as a velvet mouse.

Tis not your will They do,—no, nor the Will
That hushes Anselm's chapel overhill.
Something that drifts in clouds, that sings in rain,
That laughs in sunlight, shudders in the pain
Of desolate seas, or broods in basking earth
Governs Their melancholy and Their mirth.

Elusive still! Elusive as my reason
For trudging woodward in or out of season
To swing the ringing ax, as year by year
The inexplicable end draws slowly near,
And, in between, to think and think about it,—
Life's puzzling dream,—deride, believe, and doubt it.

But if I leave her seriously alone
She comes quite near, preëmpts some woodland stone,
Spreads out her kirtle like a shimmering dress
And fills my mind's remorseful emptiness
With marvelous jewels made of words and wit
Till all my being sings because of it,

Sings of the way her bronze hair waves about
And how her amber-lighted eyes peer out;
Sings of her sudden laughter floating wild,
Of all her antics of a fairy child,
Of her uplifted head and swift, demure
Silence and awe, than purity more pure.

So I must scratch my head and drop my ax,
While in her hands my will is twisted wax;
So, when she goes, deaf, dumb and blind I sit
Watching her empty arm-chair opposite,
Witched by evasive brightness in the brain
That grows full glory when she comes again.

JOYCE KILMER
1886-1918

Poets

Vain is the chiming of forgotten bells
    That the wind sways above a ruined shrine.
Vainer his voice in whom no longer dwells
    Hunger that craves immortal Bread and Wine.

Light songs we breathe that perish with our breath
    Out of our lips that have not kissed the rod.
They shall not live who have not tasted death;
    They only sing who are struck dumb by God.

Trees

I think that I shall never see
A poem lovely as a tree.

A tree whose hungry mouth is pressed
Against the earth's sweet flowing breast;

A tree that looks at God all day
And lifts her leafy arms to pray;

A tree that may in summer wear
A nest of robins in her hair;

Upon whose bosom snow has lain;
Who intimately lives with the rain.

Poems are made by fools like me,
But only God can make a tree.

EDNA ST. VINCENT MILLAY
1892-1950

God's World

O world, I cannot hold thee close enough!
　Thy winds, thy wide grey skies!
　Thy mists, that roll and rise!
Thy woods, this autumn day, that ache and sag
And all but cry with colour! That gaunt crag
To crush! To lift the lean of that black bluff!
World, World, I cannot get thee close enough!

Long have I known a glory in it all,
　　But never knew I this;
　　Here such a passion is
As stretcheth me apart,—Lord, I do fear
Thou'st made the world too beautiful this year;
My soul is all but out of me,—let fall
No burning leaf; prithee, let no bird call.

Afternoon on a Hill

I will be the gladdest thing
　Under the sun!
I will touch a hundred flowers
　And not pick one.

I will look at cliffs and clouds
　With quiet eyes,
Watch the wind bow down the grass,
　And the grass rise.

And when lights begin to show
    Up from the town,
I will mark which must be mine,
    And then start down!

Three Songs of Shattering

I

The first rose on my rose-tree
    Budded, bloomed, and shattered,
During sad days when to me
    Nothing mattered.

Grief of grief has drained me clean;
    Still it seems a pity
No one saw,—it must have been
    Very pretty.

II

Let the little birds sing;
    Let the little lambs play;
Spring is here; and so 'tis spring;—
    But not in the old way!

I recall a place
    Where a plum-tree grew;
There you lifted up your face,
    And blossoms covered you.

If the little birds sing,
    And the little lambs play,
Spring is here; and so 'tis spring—
    But not in the old way!

III

All the dog-wood blossoms are underneath the tree!
    Ere spring was going—ah, spring is gone!
And there comes no summer to the like of you and me,—
    Blossom time is early, but no fruit sets on.

All the dog-wood blossoms are underneath the tree,
    Browned at the edges, turned in a day;
And I would with all my heart they trimmed a mound
        for me,
    And weeds were tall on all the paths that led that way!

The Dream

Love, if I weep it will not matter,
    And if you laugh I shall not care;
Foolish am I to think about it,
    But it is good to feel you there.

Love, in my sleep I dreamed of waking,—
    White and awful the moonlight reached
Over the floor, and somewhere, somewhere,
    There was a shutter loose,—it screeched!

Swung in the wind,—and no wind blowing!—
    I was afraid, and turned to you,
Put out my hand to you for comfort,—
    And you were gone! Cold, cold as dew,

Under my hand the moonlight lay!
    Love, if you laugh I shall not care,
But if I weep it will not matter,—
    Ah, it is good to feel you there!

Ashes of Life

Love has gone and left me and the days are all alike;
    Eat I must, and sleep I will,—and would that night were here!
But ah!—to lie awake and hear the slow hours strike!
    Would that it were day again!—with twilight near!

Love has gone and left me and I don't know what to do;
    This or that or what you will is all the same to me;
But all the things that I begin I leave before I'm through,—
    There's little use in anything as far as I can see.

Love has gone and left me,—and the neighbors knock and borrow,
    And life goes on forever like the gnawing of a mouse,—
And to-morrow and to-morrow and to-morrow and to-morrow
    There's this little street and this little house.